BARRIERS TO LOVING

Barriers to Loving is an intriguing exploration of the role of sexual love over the course of life. Beginning with the mental health profession's avoidance of the topic, Levine proposes a compendium of love's pathologies by reorganizing what is familiar to clinicians into the barriers that limit the formation of adult–adult love, impediments that diminish a partner's lovability, and the impediments to feeling and expressing love for a partner. Before reviewing scientific contributions to the understanding of love, he explores the topics of sexual excess and infidelity, and how they relate to the aspiration to love and be loved. The final two chapters synthesize with clarity what to teach about love to young professionals in order to prepare them for the complexities they will soon encounter, and provide a sophisticated answer to the question, "What is love?" *Barriers to Loving* integrates humanism, science, and clinical experience in Levine's long-appreciated unique and mature voice.

Stephen B. Levine, MD, is clinical professor of psychiatry at Case Western Reserve University School of Medicine. He is the author of *Sex is Not Simple*, *Sexual Life: A Clinician's Guide*, *Sexuality in Midlife*, and *Demystifying Love: Plain Talk for the Mental Health Professional*. He is the senior editor of the *Handbook of Clinical Sexuality for Mental Health Professionals*. He has been teaching, providing clinical care, and writing since 1973. He is codirector of the Center for Marital and Sexual Health in Beachwood, Ohio. He is a recipient of the Society for Sex Therapy and Research's Masters and Johnson's Award for Lifetime Achievement.

BARRIERS TO LOVING

A Clinician's Perspective

Stephen B. Levine

NEW YORK AND LONDON

First published 2014
by Routledge
711 Third Avenue, New York, NY 10017

and by Routledge
27 Church Road, Hove, East Sussex BN3 2FA

Routledge is an imprint of the Taylor & Francis Group, an informa business

Library of Congress Cataloging-in-Publication Data

Levine, Stephen B., 1942–
Barriers to loving : a clinician's perspective / Stephen B. Levine.
    pages cm
    Includes bibliographical references and index.
  1. Intimacy (Psychology)   2. Love—Psychological aspects.   3. Interpersonal relations—Psychological aspects.   4. Attachment behavior.   5. Sexual disorders.   I. Title.
    BF575.I5L48 2014
    152.4'1—dc23
    2013019395

ISBN: 978-0-415-70885-2 (hbk)
ISBN: 978-0-415-70886-9 (pbk)
ISBN: 978-1-315-88589-6 (ebk)

Typeset in Goudy
by Apex CoVantage, LLC

SUSTAINABLE
FORESTRY
INITIATIVE

Certified Sourcing
www.sfiprogram.org
SFI-00555
The SFI label applies to the text stock.

Printed and bound in the United States of America by
Walsworth Publishing Company, Marceline, MO.

TO THOSE WHO STILL SEEK TO
UNDERSTAND

CONTENTS

PREFACE

It has been four decades since my first major academic responsibility, the development of a curriculum on human sexuality for medical students. While I was preparing for my six-lecture offering, word got out that there was an expert in sexual problems at University Hospitals of Cleveland. Within a month of completing my residency, my half-time private practice was filled with men, women, and couples with diverse difficulties, most of which I had not previously seen. In those days, my apparent credential was that I had twice read Masters and Johnson's 1966 and 1970 books, had skimmed the Kinsey volumes, and had three years of reading Freud. I had wonderful mentors to consult with who were not knowledgeable about sexual dysfunction. I was alone with my inexperience and could only laugh at my awareness that my expertise was a product of my patients' imaginations. What I actually had was the thrilling opportunity to participate in a newly opened arena of treatment. I began as a sex doctor and, as tawdry as that phrase may seem in ordinary language, it afforded me an opportunity to immerse myself in these problems and to interact with other "experts" in eastern seaboard university settings. We were all beginners, quasi-acolytes of first Masters and Johnson, then Helen Kaplan and Harold Leif.

Over the years, clinical sexuality has come to encompass not only an expanded list of sexual dysfunctions, but also sexual identity issues involving gender identity, orientation, paraphilia, and relationship discord. The enterprise has vastly expanded into urology and gynecology, where medical and surgical interventions and studies predominate; into psychology, where sexual behaviors are studied and given therapy; into psychiatry, where medications affecting sexual function are manipulated; into the pharmaceutical industry, where prosexual medications are developed and tested; and into politics, where sexual minority stakeholders and critics of the medicalization of sexual life exert their influences. It is a far cry from the world I thought I was describing for medical students in 1974.

I long ago gave up the label of sex doctor. I passed through several temporary identities, alighting at the label of being a specialist in the broad range of human sexual concerns. I consider an expert to be a person who knows enough about a subject to know what is known and, more importantly, what is not known. I watched many colleagues develop a true expertise in one or more of the many problems within this range of concerns. These individuals have taught me much from their scholarly delving into their topics.

While I am still greatly interested in sexual life and its problems, my interests have been veering towards the commonalities of problems. I have always been more interested in the nature of clinical topics, such as sexual desire, paraphilia, psychological intimacy, infidelity, etc., than how to do therapy for the dilemmas stemming from them. I earn my living through therapy, of course, but this search for what is beneath has long characterized my thinking.

It is through following this theme of commonalities that I became preoccupied with love as a topic. Like others, I have had to come to grips with love's nature as seen in my psyche, my wife's, and my children's behaviors. Never one to rigidly separate my personal experiences from my clinical ones, always tempted to compare my patients' stories to my own, and unable to escape references to love everywhere from highbrow to lowbrow culture, I eventually became astounded that my field avoided the subject. I went into psychiatry thinking it best combined my youthful interests in biology, medicine, and the humanities. I still do, even though it seems to be less so than ever. But I am getting older and do not want to lament the passing of the good old days. Everything, including me, changes.

This book represents my deliberations on the topic of love. It is one essay in ten parts. It is what I think after 40 years of immersion in subjective personal and interpersonal suffering. I cannot realistically hope to write another reflection on the nature of love twenty years from now. But if am judged to be a somewhat reasonable and tolerable gadfly, others may take up the topic without embarrassment. They will improve the taxonomy, sharpen the distinctions, and add erudition by an improved integration of relevant ideas from the humanities and basic and clinical sciences. Perhaps one day it will not seem disreputable to refer to oneself as a love doctor.

There are many avenues of learning. Science is but one of them. When it comes to deepening our understanding of love, we must be open to the contributions of many.

Stephen B. Levine, MD
April 2013

1

THE AVOIDANCE OF LOVE

The complex multifaceted processes of love are relevant to our emotional and physical lives throughout the life cycle. They begin with the investment in pregnancy, move to being cared for during infancy and childhood, and transition into adolescent sexual explorations of the self and the other during courtships. They progress through deepening attachment, commitment, and ultimately the largest challenge—harmoniously sharing lives throughout adulthood, including the care of a deteriorating partner. Failing at these adult challenges, which is quite common, often leads to profound disappointment, demoralization, anxiety, depression, alienation, motivation to avoid partner sex, infidelity, divorce, and isolation, or starting over with a new partner. Many of the complaints brought to mental health professionals ultimately prove to be the consequence of these relationship failures. Although it often goes unrecognized, mental health professionals deal with the casualties of love.

Conspicuous and subtle impediments to successful adult love processes are continuously illustrated in literature, television, theater and film, and in other branches of the humanities—but not in the mental health professions! We only occasionally mention the topic. We debate the ideal classification of psychiatric disorders and even sexual dysfunctions without acknowledging that they often are impediments to providing and receiving love.

Why We Avoid the Topic of Love

Many forces converge to create the tradition of avoidance. Avoidance begins with what culture and the mental health professions see as our responsibility. The domain of the mental health professions encompasses disturbances of thinking, feeling, perception, and behavior. These disturbances are generically referred to as psychopathology and are codified into our DSM and ICD nosologies. Basic clinical training and continuing education in all disciplines revolve around these disorders.

Difficulties negotiating the processes of love at any stage of life may create the pathways to mental disturbances or exacerbate already existent ones, but they do not constitute the actual disturbance. In many settings, a patient's treatment for

1

depression after a failed romance may focus only on anxiety and depressive symptoms. When individuals with existing psychopathology fail at love's processes, our interest often remains in their psychopathology rather than in what went wrong, and why and what we can do to help them to succeed in the future. Most individuals attempt to court and to share a sexual life with another adult. When their failure leads to a mental health evaluation, the source of their disturbance is often perceived in terms other than the failure: the diagnosis; character pathology; early development; conditioning processes; poor coping skills; abnormal brain chemistry; genes; dysfunctional neural circuitry; and gene-environment interactions. These etiologic concepts create very different ways of understanding the patient's frustration in love. They offer alternate vocabularies to describe symptoms and separate therapeutic approaches. The failure at love quickly is overlooked.

The Difference between Etiology and Pathogenesis

Etiologic concepts about the sources of psychopathology aim to describe the essential causes of the condition for all of those who have the disorder. For example, the question, "What is the cause of Major Depressive Disorder?" seeks to define the diatheses to the diagnosis. "Loss" is said to be a common precipitant. Since most mental conditions are thought to be multi-determined, clinicians assume that the source is more complicated and seek more remote diatheses. Another approach is possible. The therapist may look for the antecedent of the loss by asking why the patient's partner ended the relationship. If a clear answer is not forthcoming, another question may better focus the inquiry on how he may have failed to accommodate her requirements, "What explains her failure to tolerate the relationship with you?" His answer then positions the therapist to ask about the antecedent of his answer. This step-wise approach to the relevant sequences of the history of the present illness both engages the patient in understanding his life and illuminates the pathogenesis of his Major Depressive Disorder. This concept of pathogenesis is quite different from modern statements about remote biological-environmental interactions as the etiology of mental illness.[1] The etiology of disorders is discussed in textbooks, research articles, and lecture halls; the pathogenesis of a patient's disorder is discussed in therapy rooms.

Modern psychiatric education in major journals and continuing education courses overwhelmingly focuses on disorders and their biological etiology. Love is left out. The predominant method taught for relieving suffering is medication. Thought leaders, however, discuss a broader individualized approach that integrates neuroscience and psychotherapy.[2] Many have commented upon the frequency with which varieties of behavioral therapy are now recommended for diverse problems.[3] Therapies that rest on the tradition of psychoanalysis are less preoccupied with biological etiology in favor of remote developmental pathogenesis. Their influence has receded in recent decades as psychiatry has dramatically shifted toward psychopharmacology and evidence-based interventions. These trends have paved the way for psychotherapeutic processes to be conducted by other mental health professionals.[4] Psychologists, social workers, counselors and others are apt to engage their patients in the processes of their individual lives and to focus on the pathogenesis of their suffering. They do not get bogged down in the biological aspects of their patients' conditions. Even they, however, do not appear to discuss the problem in terms of failures at love's processes. They, too, have been acculturated to steer clear of love. They find other paradigms—such as, trauma, anxiety, depression, aggression, stigmatization, etc., for understanding the source of suffering.

Why Not Love?

It is useful to explore the numerous reasons that love is not used as a starting point for understanding the pathogenesis of emotional disturbances. Avoidance of the topic may be based on assumptions about the nature of love. If professionals assume that love is merely an abstraction, an ideal, a naïve youthful ambition or an illusion, then the topic will seem irrelevant to the mission to understand and relieve mental suffering. The French psychoanalyst-philosopher Jacques Lacan articulated this viewpoint when he said, "Love is giving something you haven't got to someone who doesn't exist."[5] Many non-clinician philosophers take the opposite view—love, while not a unitary or easily definable term, is vital, nonetheless, to understanding human life processes.[6] My view is that concepts of love and its processes are essential to the mission of mental health professionals, and so the question of why we avoid these topics so persistently is worth exploring. I suspect that eight additional factors play a role.

1. **Professionalism**: All professions create an exclusive vocabulary that adds to their mystique, making it difficult for others to easily understand. Failed love processes as pathways to suffering are too easily understood by nonprofessionals and consequently rob mental health professionals of the claim to specialized knowledge.
2. **Duty**: We perceive that our major responsibility is to retrieve patients from their overwhelmed states rather than to primarily focus on the processes that devastated them. Thus, many of our modern therapies aim to cope with symptoms.
3. **Science**: The private, idiosyncratic, subjective processes of love are intuitively felt to be beyond the grasp of science. We want to believe that the basis of our work is scientific, so we talk about issues that can be measured and use questionnaires with Likert scales. We prefer to believe that science has previously demonstrated the merit of our current interventions. And if not science, then clinical tradition has legitimized our work. We refer to our work as being one of the clinical sciences.
4. **Ubiquity**: In partnered lives, heterosexual or homosexual, private subjective and interpersonal dramas inevitably occur that disappoint and change life possibilities. Except in egregious cases, we do not actually know where to draw the line between seriously disturbed and normal relationship

dissatisfaction. We are less uneasy with definable psychopathology than the subtle forms of the evolution of love.

5.   **Distance**: Therapists' love processes are often fraught with concern, inadequacy, and disappointment. We also fail at love's processes. We need to create distance from our personal issues in our work.

6.   **Epiphenomenon**: We assume that love problems typically are products of underlying more subtle individual developmental forces. The details of the patient's love processes are not as germane to us as the deeper issues that we prefer to discuss.

7.   **Language**: Although we have numerous schools of thought within the mental health professions, each with its own vocabulary, we lack a paradigm that does justice to the complexity of love's processes. Our paradigms focus on individuals while love's processes involve two people. We lack the language to describe the crucial private processes of: adult attachment, responding to interpersonal conflicts, developing clearer perceptions of the partner, and deepening one's understanding of the role of love in one's life. We are relatively inchoate in the face of love's evolution over the life cycle.

8.   **Maturation**: The importance of love may only come into focus after we master the tasks of basic mental health education and accumulate enough experience to realize the limitations of our paradigms. We may then actually begin to address the obviously relevant topic in our own manner. But because of these 10 other factors, we do not often talk with colleagues about how we focus on love. Instead, we talk together about relationship issues, character problems, childhood trauma, a diagnosis, etc. in a manner that implies that these forces interfere with current and future love. These topics seem to stand in for love.

How We Discuss Love

Modern mental health professionals do sometimes discuss love—either obliquely or through surrogate paradigms. Excellent psychiatric inpatient and outpatient care is said to be a form of love.[7] During conferences on sexual disorders, a clinician may point out in passing that our task is to enable those with sexual problems to have a more loving relationship.[8] Many clinicians regard paraphilia as courtship disorders, meaning that these conditions are obstacles to establishing a loving attachment to another person.[9] Relationship behaviors that predict future divorce (affective escalation during conflict and removing oneself from further discussion) have been well defined by behavioral scientists.[10] Psychodynamic writers periodically have taken on the task of explaining how love fails. Their work generates theoretical paradigms such as internalized objects and levels of differentiation.[11,12] These paradigms build upon other seminal contributions over the last century. Even decades before Bowlby suggested that adult love problems may have their origins in early life attachment styles,[13] Erikson wrote about the importance of love when he described the dialectical tensions between genital intimacy and isolation that had to be mastered during young adulthood to avoid significant negative consequences.[14] Earlier pioneers discussed love/lust splits (Madonna/Whore complexes) and emphasized the power of childhood psycho-sexual processes to limit adult love.[15]

Kernberg has been a contemporary source of important conceptualizations about the causes of love's failures. He has written for decades on the psychology of love through the lens of character pathologies and their underlying identity difficulties that limit the capacity to love. He posits that without such impediments, love holds the potential for an ever-deepening passionate sexual bond between two respectful autonomous individuals. While stressing the inseparable nature of aggression and love, he frequently finds explanations for love's failures in individual pre-Oedipal and Oedipal processes.[16] Although mindful of the potential impact of the characteristics of partners, he is relatively silent about their contributions to his patients' inability to sustain love.[17] Psychoanalytic investigations of patients have had an enormous influence in creating the assumption that all love problems are epiphenomena of prior individual developmental processes.

Couples therapists directly experience the interaction of two people's behaviors, meanings, values, expectations, and capacities.[18] Their work has the advantages of greater sociologic diversity and immersion in the immediacy of couples' interactions. What they do with these advantages varies because of their diverse paradigms. Historically, couples therapists have under-focused on the couple's sexual life; they tend to leave this aspect of love to the sex therapists. In a recent book, 14 sex therapy experts described how they individually deal with low sexual desire—none of them directly mentioned love.[19]

Many factors seem to be omitted by our current approaches. Marriage is often the normative assumption even though unmarried cohabitation is common throughout the life cycle in the United States and Europe. The assumption of marriage tends to bypass considerations of the struggles to love and be loved within sexual minority communities as well as the arrangements that are coming to be known as polyamory. Europe seems to be far ahead of the United States in downplaying marriage. This may reflect a greater cultural skepticism and pessimism about its potential for stability and fulfillment. The quality of the parents' marriage and the fact of their divorce lurk behind the adult's approach to courtship and romance. This tends to get lost when focusing on remote individual dynamics. These factors, at least for me, come together at a level that is not often heard when love's problems are discussed. Adults have deeply private values and beliefs about relationships. These are not to be deduced from public expressions of support for marriage and fidelity. They are often carefully hidden from others, including the future or current spouse. Clinical sophistication requires an awareness of the values that organize individual's behaviors.

Our professional choices for dealing with love often seem to me to range between paradigm-heavy speculations about early life individual processes or ignoring the topic and focusing instead on surrogate topics for love—that is, sexual, relationship, or DSM-defined symptomatic patterns. I wonder if it is possible and useful to reintroduce love to our mental health dialogues.

The Purpose of this Book

The current mental health professions do not evidence a widespread interest in or grasp of love. As represented in our research, writings, or continuing education, our work often seems largely irrelevant to love's vicissitudes and outcomes. Professionals, like laypersons, learn about and experience the complexity of love's evolution through their own experience and through novels, book reviews, movies, plays, and television comedies and dramas. Nonetheless, we continue to posit our theories about past childhood experiences determining love's possibilities. Love's adult developmental processes are far more complicated and less often conceptualized. Ultimately, our inability to grasp love's ordinary complexity and individuality may be the central reason why we professionals avoid love. We may be fundamentally embarrassed by the fact that we, too, are taught about love by creative people outside of our field.

This volume is a search for answers about love. The most basic question, "What is love?" underlies every other question about love. If we deemed it important, what would we teach our trainees about love, its problems, its archetypal psychopathologies, and how concepts of love can be effectively used in psychotherapy?

Current mental health perspectives on love have some utility and validity. They tend to be so basic as to orient students to intrapsychic process in general. Erikson's concepts about developmental tasks and the evolution of developmental lines over time provide a crucial orientation to love's processes. He pointed out that individuals had to master numerous intrapsychic forces to establish a loving sexual relationship and then to maintain a harmonious relationship as they mature and cope with life's diverse demands. The consequences of failing at these tasks were to prevent future development that rested upon their accomplishment.

Traditional and modern concepts about love that are familiar to mental health professionals need to be placed within the larger social context clarified by scholars and other creative thinkers. This book aims to integrate knowledge from other fields so that mental health professionals can gain confidence that they can and should share their perspectives with some of their patients. After all, when we provide opportunities for patients to talk to us at length over time, most of the conversation centers on their concerns about their primary adult intimate relationship—in this way, they talk about love. Therapists want to be helpful. The ever-present question is how to be so. This book suggests that we need to refine our understanding of love and have the courage to use that understanding to assist patients in their struggles to obtain and maintain the stabilizing influences of love. As ideas about love are discussed in the book, we need to be aware of their limitations as well as their strengths. Knowledge about love is not different from knowledge in general. In any field of inquiry, it is difficult to establish a fact and discern organizing principles. Science is only one way of establishing facts and deducing organizing principles. The hoped for lasting consequence of this book to is make the dialogue of psychotherapy more relevant to patient sensibilities. Can we improve our helpfulness by returning to the topic of love?

References

1 Baram, T.D. (2012). Fragmentation and unpredictability of early-life experience in mental disorders. *American Journal of Psychiatry, 169*(9), 907–915.

2 Gabbard, G. (2005). Mind, brain, and personality disorders. *American Journal of Psychiatry, 162*(4), 648–655.

3 Jeste, D. (2012). 2012 Presidential Address. American Psychiatric Association Annual Meeting. Philadelphia.

4 West, J.P. (2012, June). Less than half of psychiatrists surveyed practice psychotherapy. *Clinical Psychiatry News*, pp. 1 and 3.

5 Phillips, A. (1994). *On flirtation: Psychoanalytic essays on the uncommitted life.* New York: Harvard University Press.

6 Singer, I. (2009). *Philosphy of love: A partial summing up.* Cambridge, Massachusetts: The MIT Press.

7 Waltos, H. (2011, 15 June). *What's love got to do with it? Love's role in psychiatry.* Retrieved from http://www.retreatatsp.org/latest-news/uncategorized/loves-role-in-psychiatry/

8 Metz M., & McCarthy B. (2011). *Enduring desire: Your guide to lifelong intimacy.* New York: Routledge.

9 Freund, K.B. (1986). The concept of courtship disorder. *Journal of Sex & Marital Therapy, 12*(2), 79–92.

10 Gottman, J.M. (1988). Psychology and the study of marital processes. *Annual Review of Psychology, 49*, 169–197.

11 Scharff, D. (1977). *Refinding the object and reclaiming the self.* Landham, Maryland: Rowman and Littlefield.

12 Schnarch, D. (1991). *The sexual crucible: Integrating sex and marital therapy.* New York: WW Norton & Co.

13 Bowlby, J. (1988). Developmental psychiatry comes of age. *American Journal of Psychiatry, 145*(1), 1–10.

14 Erikson, E.H. (1963). *Childhood and society* (2nd ed.). New York, NY: WW Norton & Company.

15 Freud, S. (1912). On the universal tendency to debasement in the sphere of love. In S. Freud, *The standard edition of the complete works of Sigmund Freud* (Vol. 11, pp. 179–190). London: Hogarth Press.

16 Kernberg, O. (2012). *The inseparable nature of love and aggression: Clinical and theoretical perspectives.* Washington, DC: American Psychiatric Publishing.

17 Kernberg, O. (2012). The psychology of sexual love. In O. Kernberg, *The inseparable nature of love and aggression: Clinical and theoretical perspectives* (pp. 247–306). Washington, DC: American Psychiatric Publishing.

18 Sager, C. (1977). *Marital contracts and couple's therapy: Hidden forces in intimate relationships.* New York: Brunner/Mazel.

19 Leiblum, S.R. (2010). *Sexual desire disorders: A casebook.* New York: Guilford.

2

A COMPENDIUM OF LOVE'S PATHOLOGIES

Can love be sick? Do love processes have healthy and sick forms? Can a previously healthy person develop a mental disorder from a disappointment in love? Can a partner's death induce an unwillingness to love again? Can mental disorders affect the capacity to love? Are there character traits that decrease lovability? Can personality traits limit the capacity to love another? Can a new couple be doomed to relationship failure by an aspect of one of their personalities? I suspect that most professionals would quickly answer these questions "yes." I continue to wonder why such observations have not organized our professional discourse on life processes and the pathogenesis and etiology of mental disorders.

One contributor to our professional avoidance of love is our meager and confusing lexicon. For example, the term lovesickness has been used for many centuries. It usually denotes a state of pining for an unavailable beloved. This longing is thought to be eradicated by getting what one wants from the beloved, reciprocally attaching to another person, or becoming interested in something considered more important. Many individuals, particularly among the young, transiently experience lovesickness. The term is usually applied to a person who is not behaving as he or she usually does. It is rare to hear someone confess to being lovesick. The label connotes a transient emotional state rather than a mental illness. Lovesick characters are often depicted in the theater.[1] Recently, lovesickness has been employed as the heading for a two-item list of psychopathologies of love that included only erotomania and psychosomatic illness.[2] I was shocked to find the term used as a heading for psychopathologies, but this reminded me that when the concept of the psychopathology of love appears in modern psychiatric writings, a forensic specialist is typically the author. The article usually describes a crime associated with psychotic distortion of courtship or paranoid jealousy.[3] Most of love's problems, of course, are not seen in forensic settings.

One need only read two authors discussing passionate love, companionate love, or true love to realize that writers are not necessarily describing the same phenomena.[4] We need to improve the lexicon of love if we are to better understand love as an avenue to emotional suffering. As a first step, we need to use phrases that convey the breadth of the spectrum of difficulties that occur in the sphere of love. Here are a series of terms with differing connotations that fulfill this criterion.

1. *Love's sicknesses* is the most casual.
2. *The psychopathologies of love* evokes a formal traditional mental disorders approach.
3. *Love's pathologies* is a bit less imposing.
4. *The impediments to love* evokes the barriers preventing love.
5. *The impediments to loving* conjure the barriers to love as a process.
6. *Barriers to love or loving* is much the same as #4 and #5.

I will employ all of these terms trying to make use of their subtle differences.

This chapter explores the reasonableness and utility of trying to develop a compendium of love's pathologies. There are reasons to suspect that a compendium is not a logical choice. For one, it has never been done. Sexual psychopathologies have been categorized in various ways for over a century, but not love's problems. While sex is relevant to the experience of love, they are not the same phenomena. Perhaps love is just too difficult a subject—too idiosyncratic—to grasp by science or scholarship. In the last analysis, love may not even lie within the province of the mental health professions. Because of its fundamental nature, perhaps it belongs to philosophy or theology. We seem to be aware that numerous external forces throughout the world shape a person's and a couple's subjective and observable relationship fate. Some of these include income, ethnicity, race, religion, education, social class, historical era, gender, orientation, and political-legal sensibilities. This understanding derives from work in sociology, economics, anthropology, history, law, and political science. A compendium to integrate studies in these diverse fields seems out of the question. At the very least, it would seem to require a lifetime of scholarship to accomplish. Besides, clinicians are not that interested in all the forces that conceptually shape the form and experience of love. We are more interested in the impediments to loving observed within individuals when many of these variables are held constant. Should we have a separate compendium for impoverished American Indians and another for those with three continuous generations of wealth? External forces sculpt different love possibilities among the Taliban, in polygamous circles, or in Ireland during the 19th century famine, for example. Can we compile a catalogue of the personal and interpersonal factors that transcend these external differences?

Is there anything universal about love, its processes, and its impediments? Although we recognize that external variables may subtly infiltrate our thoughts, feelings, perceptions, and values during the course of our lives, the challenge for a compendium is to organize love's personal and interpersonal variables in terms understood by clinicians. The complexity of all of this interaction makes the idea of a compendium seem to be an unreasonable endeavor. When we consider that love is understood to be simultaneously mysterious and obvious, predictable and unpredictable, conscious and unconscious, and individual and interactive, construction of a compendium would seem doomed from the start.

Nonetheless, it may be reasonable to think about compiling a compendium of love's barriers if we confine the concept to the issues that clinicians see and bear responsibility for in our current roles. Relative to the above, a compendium will be a modest catalogue. It would not pretend to scientific vigor. Its early form will be a thought experiment without statistical validation. The experiment would be an attempt to explore whether the mental health professions need to upgrade the topic of love in our professional discourse. It asks the question: Can a compendium be helpful to therapists and those they serve? It will certainly not be the last word on the subject. If it has any heuristic value, others will improve upon its content and its organization. While it is my hope that a compendium will increase our ability to see the significance of what is routinely now before our eyes, the final decision about whether it adds anything to our professional lives will have to lie with the reader.

Initial Problems Establishing a Compendium

During the early months of trying to formulate a compendium, a series of challenges became apparent. The first was the question, "How to generically define what constitutes a pathology of love?" I decided that the solution was to delineate the characteristics of a person that impede the formation of an attachment or deteriorate one that had formed. This decision led to the second task of how to make order of the numerous pathologies of love that I could conceptualize. The diversity created a muddled mixture of perspectives until I realized that they naturally fell into three divisions:

1. Impediments to Establishing a Loving Relationship
2. Impediments that Diminish the Person's Lovability
3. Impediments that Limit the Person's Ability to Express Love

Even with this division into three major categories, each category was challenged by the diverse natures of what was listed. A psychiatric diagnosis, the motivation to avoid being hurt again, poor organization skills, and fear of one's own hostility are given equal weights in the listings. I decided that diversity of impediments was what existed and had to be accepted.

Two related additional problems became apparent when I shared an early version with colleagues. Some individuals thought I was proposing an alternative to our official nosology. This surprised me since I thought it was clear that I was suggesting that some psychiatric diagnoses impeded the processes of loving. It had not occurred to me that the compendium would be viewed as hostile criticism even though my view was that our nosology did not directly address problematic patterns of love and did not recognize the significance of psychiatric disorders to the adult attachment processes. While I have noticed that many marital therapists ignore nosology in their work, I was not suggesting an alternative nosology. These criticisms were correct in that I was suggesting that DSM-5 and its predecessors reflected our professional avoidance of love.

Other colleagues noted that the focus on the pathologies of love was phenotypic or surface-oriented. They preferred dealing directly with the depth of understanding of life processes that their favorite theories provided. I think these comments were polite dismissals of the utility of the compendium because of its superficiality. Medical students studying histopathology are taught a method for determining the evaluation of a slide containing a sliver of tissue. The first step is to examine the slide with the naked eye. What tissue could it be? The next steps are to examine it under low, medium, and high power—in that order. In this way, students are far more likely to correctly identify the pathological state of the organ component they are studying. Later in life, I extended the discipline to psychopathology. Clinically, students are also taught not to bypass a close visual inspection of the patient. I don't disrespect the surface of things; they can reveal much to the observant eye. The description of the compendium as superficial made me realize that I had to be compellingly clear in explaining the categories in each of the three divisions to avoid offending psychiatric political and ideological sensibilities.

The final challenge came from the realization that I was creating a compendium of love's problems without a clear understanding of what we mean by love. I have long been aware that most of the writers who invoke the noun or verb form of love presume that their readers know what they mean by the word. I did not want to commit the same error, so I committed myself to explaining how items in the compendium interfered with love's known processes. This commitment made me realize that a book was required to explore this subject because concepts about adult sexual love derive from theology, philosophy, psychology and research in the social sciences. It would take a considerable space to integrate these scholarly endeavors. Labeling a person's characteristic as a psychopathology of love meant that it would have to be clear how that trait impairs the emotions of pleasure, interest, and sexual motivation. I was hoping it could at least be a short book.

The Compendium

The remainder of this chapter will provide a quick overview of each of the three divisions of the compendium. Rather than having an extensive discussion of the subcategories in each division, emphasis will be placed on the division as a whole. More extensive descriptions of the subcategories will be provided in the three subsequent chapters.

Part 1: Impediments to Establishing a Loving Relationship

One definition of love recognizes that it is an arrangement between two people, a deal that they make after assessing one another during courtship. The arrangement has immediate and continuing physical, emotional, and social consequences that may ultimately lead to a deeper bond. It is suffused with culture's lofty ambitions that each mate will accompany, assist, and enrich the individuals as they evolve through expected and unexpected life changes.[5] Many of the items in Part 1 prevent, impede, or change the nature of the deal that is verbally, nonverbally, and unconsciously struck between them.

In viewing the items in Part 1, it is helpful to realize that courtship, which many of us associate with the young, occurs at every stage of adulthood and involve the unmarried, the divorced, the widowed, and those seeking an affair. The impediments have separate meanings for the individual and his or her potential mate. Courtship is the process whereby these meanings are defined and transformed into relationship enhancing or relationship curtailing behaviors.

The presence of an impediment, per se, does not preclude the formation of a loving bond. It only diminishes its likelihood, limits the field of possible mates, or changes the terms of the deal that will be struck. Skepticism about the new relationships of others is often based on the idea that the individuals have exercised poor judgment—either an individual has failed to appreciate the actual incapacities of the partner or has failed to realize the long-term effects of the burden of dealing with the partner's impediment. Whether this skepticism is correct or erroneous, clinicians are reminded that early love arrangements are accompanied by the imagination of a new, enhanced, and wonderful interpersonal life.

The first seven categories in the list of Impediments to Establishing a Loving Relationship are fairly conspicuous features that soon become apparent during the vetting process of courtship. The impediments in the final category (H), however, are subtle. The last one, the so-called Love/Lust split, most clearly earns the label of a psychopathology of love.

A. Major Physical Disabilities: e.g., paraplegia, hemophilia, obesity
B. Major Cognitive Disabilities: e.g., developmental intellectual disabilities, autism, traumatic brain injury
C. Major Mental Illness: e.g., schizophrenia, major mood disorder, alcoholism or other addictions, anorexia nervosa, obsessive-compulsive disorder, other psychoses such as paranoid jealousy, erotomania, stalking
D. Gender Identity Disorders or Gender Dysphoria
E. Character Pathology: e.g., conspicuous paranoid, narcissistic, borderline or psychopathic behaviors
F. Select Paraphilias: e.g., pedophilia, exhibitionism, voyeurism
G. Lifelong Sexual Dysfunctions—the specific dysfunction is not as important as its persistence but they include: aversion; lack of sexual interest in partner; inability to be aroused by sexual behavior with partner; inability to attain orgasm with a partner; vaginismus (causing non-consummation); dyspareunia (precluding future genital union). Partnership can be based, however, on the lack of sexual activity or with sexual activity without sexual intercourse. This creates a crisis when pregnancy is desired.

H. Courtship Disappointments

1. Recurrent pattern of falling in love with the unreachable, unavailable, or those who are not even aware.
2. Rejection—may result when individuals enjoy each other to different degrees and have different plans for their futures. Rejected persons may avoid the possibility of another relationship for long periods of time. The rejecting person may only participate in courtship for sexual experience.
3. Refusal to commit to marriage. Some individuals feel strongly that they will not and should not marry although they participate in relationship building until the point of public and legal commitment. They run at commitment time.
4. Patterned loss of sexual interest in increasingly committed relationships (the form of acquired Hypoactive Sexual Desire Disorder that is known as Love/Lust Split or Madonna/Whore complex). This pattern tends to baffle unsuspecting partners, the individuals whose desire has disappeared, and their therapists.

Although when stated it seems obvious, clinicians are not used to stressing that physical and psychiatric disorders are impediments to making a loving attachment. The danger of this professional oversight is that when psychiatric patients suffer the consequences of living without a caring intimate adult connection, therapists may misattribute their sadness, loneliness, or intoxication to their disorder rather than to their inability to find a mate and fall in love. An increase in their medication is not usually helpful.

Although three of the four courtship disappointments are not recognized disorders, they share a crippling fear of attachment. Motivation to protect oneself may ultimately stem from remote or recent previous attachments.[6] Fear of attachment may underlie many of the items in Part 1. Even though the symptomatic presentations are different within its eight categories, the pathogeneses may not be entirely separate.

Part 2: Impediments That Diminish the Person's Lovability

This division of the compendium focuses on the forces that undermine an established relationship. It is concerned with the characteristics that make a person less lovable. The term index person will be used to clarify that he or she is the source of the behavior, but our interest is in the partner's perception of that behavior. We are trying to look at the index person through the eyes of the partner. Sometimes the index person is our patient. Sometimes it is the partner of our patient.

Adult love is conditional. Bestowal of support, affection, cooperation, sexual interplay, and caring are the result of a partner's appraisal of the how the index person is at home and in the world over time.[7] Bestowal once withdrawn because of bad behavior can be restored by forgiveness, but continuation of the regained harmony is predicated on the problematic behavior not recurring. Recurrent

13

disappointing behavior tends to devitalize the union, although the partner may save the relationship for its social, economic, or child-rearing benefits. This may appear to outsiders as a self-sacrificing love devoted to the well-being of others, a form of love known theologically as agape.[8] Therapists see that such relationships are often characterized by diminutions in pleasure in presence of the partner, interest in the partner's activities, respect for the person, sexual desire for the partner, willingness to assist the partner, and optimism about the value of their future as a couple. These are aspects of the partner's inability to remain wholeheartedly invested in the relationship. This division of the compendium reminds us that there is an unseen process in the partner shaping an index person's fate. If love has the potential to grow stronger over time even as its sexual intensity lessens, Part 2's barriers to loving not only prevent this growth, they also deteriorate the bond that previously was achieved. They often permanently put love's evolution on a less pleasurable developmental trajectory.

A. Incompatible Sexual Identity Variations—the harmony of a relationship is profoundly disturbed by a person who announces the emergence of a wish to change sex or a redefinition of the self into another orientation. The partner experiences this as personal rejection and anticipates abandonment.

B. Acquired Sexual Dysfunctions—These patterns deprive a partner of the nonverbal visceral process of reaffirming the pleasures of their bond and can increase hostility and decrease forbearance. They risk the permanent loss of sexual activity, depression/anxiety, termination of the relationship, or extra-dyadic sex. The risks are greater in young and middle-aged couples. While some of these dysfunctions can have a significant biological contribution, any of these presentations can be psychogenic. New dysfunctions may be manifested by: aversion, loss of desire, loss of arousability, early ejaculation, anorgasmia, or dyspareunia.

C. Sexual Excess Patterns involving combinations of masturbation, commercial sex, pornography, extramarital relationships, or Internet sexual socialization profoundly strain a partner's ability to remain in the relationship. The discovery of the sexual excess usually just adds to the partner's burden that already may have been compromised by what clinicians call comorbidities—such as hypomania/mania, substance abuse, addiction proneness, mood/anxiety disorders, and attention deficit disorders. When some sexual excess patterns are effectively dealt with, the sick role afforded to the person in treatment mitigates the risk of immediate, but not future, termination of the relationship.

D. Paraphilias can either dominate the personal and interpersonal behaviors of the patient or be associated with normal sexual function without using the paraphilic script. Either group can erode a loving relationship as the paraphilic needs come to dominate sex. Fetishism, sadism, masochism, pedophilia, and transvestism are commonly clinically seen to impair an existing relationship.

E. Character Traits That Alienate. Therapists have innumerable schemes for explaining how relationships deteriorate over time. My current preferences are to think about many problematic behaviors as based on character traits that induce alienation. Others may prefer to emphasize struggles involving power, control, or gender roles; or to stress unrealistic expectations and intimacy barriers; or to focus on theoretical underpinnings of these traits. However this category is described, clinicians will note its complexity and incompleteness. In devising the subcategories for Character Traits That Alienate, I was governed by the idea that each partner is constantly weighing alternate meanings of the partner's behavior. Negative appraisals can come from both specific disapproved of behaviors as well as a growing awareness of the limits of the partner's capacities.

1. Recurrent inability to problem-solve together
2. Unacceptable differences in honesty, religiosity, political sensibilities
3. Fatigue from managing differing cultural interests and pleasures
4. Differing concepts of what are acceptable boundaries for the relationship—e.g., friendship patterns, flirtation, extra-dyadic sex
5. Realization of the partner's limited endowment of emotional expressiveness, intelligence, vocational effort, sexual capacity, athleticism, or interest in others
6. Gradual realization of divergent life goals

F. Aggressive Behaviors. A partner's aggressiveness within the relationship is a great challenge to bestowal of love. Clinicians learn about verbally abusive demeaning dominance patterns, sexual demandingness, refusal to cooperate with divorce through passive-aggressive or directly uncooperative, thwarting, and delaying behaviors. Clinicians learn about the most egregious forms of aggressiveness, however, through the media when crimes are reported or when perpetrators are dealt with by the judicial system. Criminal aggressiveness includes: sexual harassment; physical abuse; stalking of the partner or others; sexual abuse of minors within or outside the family; and threat of or actual murder in response to a partner's intention to divorce or a partner's worsening jealous state.

G. New Major Mental or Physical Illness—The onset of serious mental or physical illness can deteriorate affection, caring, sexual expression, and commitment in couples that previously had seemingly good-enough relationships. The index person's loss of functional capacity and increasing self-centeredness and the burden of caring for the impaired person exceed the partner's capacity. Through these forces, the illness converts a previous good-enough deal into a poor arrangement.

H. Other Sources of the Loss of Love—Partners have certain standards for bestowal of kindness, affection, and sexual access that are realized only after these standards are not maintained. They are violated by the inability to remain cordial to family, infidelity, criminality, and refusal to affectively participate in the relationship.

"For better or worse, in sickness and in health" sounds lovely at ceremonies. The "worse" cannot be imagined until it presents itself. The reactions to these adversities are not entirely predictable because they are filtered through the unique sensibilities of the partner. When I look at Part 2 as a whole, I am awed by all that must be unseen and unspoken within the partner in order to act lovingly to the index person. The partner does not necessarily feel pleasure, interest, or desire yet acts with patience, kindness, and understanding. Loving the partner is a self-management process.

Part 3: Impediments That Limit the Person's Ability to Express Love

Part 3 is the most difficult division of the compendium to understand. It requires a shift in perspective. It is not primarily concerned with the partner's behavior but with the mental processes that affect the index person. We are now trying to comprehend the forces that limit the index person's capacity to experience and express love to a partner. Of course, the index person can withdraw his or her love from the partner because of negative appraisals based on the factors just described in Part 2 factors. While Part 3 is more concerned with forces that have little to do with the partner, it is impossible to be certain that Part 3 factors have nothing to do with the partner. A partner may have similar traits throughout life but numerous subtle maturational shifts occur in the index person to change the person's judgments about the partner. Part 3 reminds us of a limitation inherent to clinically describing partnered life: the difficulty separating the personal from interpersonal.

Terms that describe emerging sensibilities about the partner are particularly difficult to label as pathologies of love because they seem to come from the partner. The index person is reacting to the partner's patterns. However, there are two factors that give us pause in accepting this at its face. First to be considered is that the descriptions of the partner's patterns may camouflage the index person's behaviors that provoked the partner. We should recall that after one or more relationship failures that were initially blamed on partners, individuals may conclude that they do not have the capacities to live harmoniously with another person. It is only then that they understand that they possess some pathology of love. We might call the pathology the inability to take responsibility for personal contributions to new problematic circumstances. Maturation converts the habit of displacement of blame to the partner into a new self-awareness.

Second is that behind the complaints about the partner lies the index person's unexamined sensibilities. Take for example the sentence, "She is so critical all the time!" Her criticism is being filtered through a sensibility that allows for little feedback for how it feels to relate to him. When a partner characterizes the index person's behavior, *You are not a generous tipper at restaurants*, a rageful retort may follow, *There you go criticizing me again!* Part 3 attempts to define what transpires within the mind of the index person that limits his or her affection for the partner.

A. Awareness of Partner's Intense Dissatisfaction may induce a grim coldness within the person when he or she learns of the partner's dissatisfaction. This only makes improvement in the relationship more difficult.

B. Discovery of One's Alternative Gender Identity or Orientation—Many persons claim continuing love for the established partner in the face of this intensifying awareness, but it usually no longer includes sexual desire for the partner. They often wish to pursue a more complete relationship with someone else. Their regret may not prevent breakup or divorce.

C. Acquired Sexual Dysfunctions—To the extent that the person perceives that the sexual dysfunction is a reflection of the loss of emotional connection to the partner, the new sexual dysfunction camouflages prior dissatisfactions with the partner. But the pathogenesis of acquired sexual dysfunctions may have nothing to do with the partner per se. Nonetheless, the dysfunction, biogenic or psychogenic, induces a defensive withdrawal from the partner and the worry that the problem means *I don't love my partner any longer.*

D. Sexual Excess Patterns—The individuals act as though they are entitled to their soothing pursuit of excitement and orgasmic comfort. While operative, they are strong barriers to providing for the needs of a partner. Clinicians seem to agree that the sexual addictions are narcissistic pursuits that contain much denial, self-hatred, low self-regard and often considerable shame.

E. Alcoholism and other forms of drug addiction—this psychopathology of love often is initially associated with blame of the partner and denial of their own unlovable behaviors.

F. Paraphilias—Like the sexual addictions, the patient's self-centered pursuit of his pleasures is associated with a loss of interest in the partner unless the partner engages in his preferred sexual scenario.

G. Problematic character traits—Ultimately, numerous inflexible behaviors that put one's own needs before those of the partner and the children are viewed as pathologies of love because they prevent the person from accurately perceiving and empathically responding to a partner. They tend to be baffling at first to the individual who cannot understand why the partner complains so much. These character-based poor adaptive capacities are the source of much interpersonal conflict and often underlie the poor prognostic behaviors described by behaviorists.

H. Aggressive behaviors—These variations of problematic character traits revolve around forcefulness, demandingness, over control, and authority and are often reinforced by the threat of or actual violence. The violence tends to escalate when the partner wants to terminate the relationship.

I. New Physical or Emotional Illness—As some people acquire new important limitations, their pain/disappointment/loss of function increases their self-preoccupation and limits their capacity to attend to the needs of their family.

J. Other Impediments—

    a.   The loss of respect for the partner because of extra-relationship sex or criminal or addictive behaviors cause a lack of willingness to be kind, cooperative, sexual, or affectionate.

    b.   Partner death or divorce can lead to unwillingness to take another risk.

    c.   A new personal interest in sexual adventuring that reflects a rejection of monogamy—sexual swinging, polyamory, unilateral exploration of Internet-acquired sexual opportunities.

As in Part 2 impediments, those in this group are not mutually exclusive. It would be ideal if the zones of demarcation between these subcategories were distinct, but they are not. It would be ideal if these ten categories had far fewer mechanisms of pathogenesis. When Part 3 impediments are viewed in their entirety, clinicians may appreciate that a harmonious enduring sexual relationship faces many obstacles, requires much intelligent self-talk and restraint, and represents a mastery over many temptations. I like to think of the ordinary processes of harmonious love as consisting of a preponderance of well handled moments that subliminally impress individuals with their partner's goodness. Occasionally, an extraordinary challenge occurs that is conspicuously well handled. This only reinforces the previous conclusion that the partner is respect worthy, valuable, and lovable. I like this concept of love's process because it sets up an understanding that an unsatisfactory relationship consists of a series of poorly handled moments punctuated by an occasional egregiously misplayed circumstance. These poorly handled situations are the basis of the stories that are told to us. While there is a great tendency to initially tell these stories about the partner's mishandling of the moments, the clinician may be more interested in how the patient views the personal mishandling of these moments. This represents an exploration of the person's sensibilities. We are interested in the meaning of events to the index person and the forces that limit his or her willingness to invest in the other.

Does this Clinical Compendium have Usefulness?

In the midst of the confusing interacting dimensions of couples' lives, I frequently point out how certain of their behaviors make it difficult for their partner to love them. I distinguish for them the crucial differences between loving a partner primarily as a moral obligation to endure the arrangement and feeling interest, pleasure, respect, and sexual desire for them over decades. I remind them that a reasonable goal to entertain is to have a partner who still profoundly loves you when you are older. These few concepts about love seem to help people grasp the importance of how they deal with today's issues and to perceive past behaviors in a new light. They seem to attenuate resistance to considering the negative impact of their contributions to the problem. Many patients grasp the relevance of the topic of love to their complaints and spontaneously comment how previous therapists never talked about love.

My practice setting attracts individuals with love and sexual concerns. Many of the patients have other emotional burdens beside those involving their primary love relationship. My setting continually stimulates my thinking about the pathogenesis of mental suffering relating to the separate aspirations to establish and maintain a harmonious love relationship. It has helped me to understand how relationships become devitalized over time, and it peaks my interest in how people preserve their mental health in the face of these impediments.

The more important issue, however, is whether the compendium can be useful to others. The usual task of a clinician is to help the patient or the couple. Understanding the pathogenesis of the problem is one of the key ingredients to being of assistance. I suggest, therefore, that clinicians ask themselves whether an impediment to bestowing or receiving love was a factor in creating their new patient's diagnosis. If so, was it the most important cause?

The compendium will be largely irrelevant in many clinical settings because the typical patient is so impaired in his or her social functioning that establishing a loving adult-adult relationship seems beyond reach. Therapists struggle with this patient to attain goals other than establishing a stabilizing affectionate enduring sexual relationship. We content ourselves with eradicating the hallucinations, lifting their depression, dissipating their frightening anger, diminishing their paralyzing anxiety about other matters or getting them to stop abusing alcohol and other drugs. Understanding such poor functioning in terms of the developmental task for attaining a reciprocal loving attachment does, however, allow the clinician to empathize with the patients' sadness over not attaining this goal. Such empathy builds trust. Understanding the compendium may also enable the clinician to explain the vetting process of courtship in terms of two people's assessment of each other's personality assets and limitations. Therapists are educators after all.

In other clinical settings, the compendium may help us to discuss the development of the patient's symptoms in a step-by-step fashion based on the history of the present illness rather than to invoke the complexity of etiology. Patients need to comprehend the avenues to their suffering. Our theoretical paradigms, no matter how skillfully we present them, are often not comprehensible to even highly educated patients as they often jump from the present to childhood or from an interpersonal dilemma to a personal deficiency. I think some patients are put off by our theories. It is my hope that understanding the compendium can keep more patients in psychotherapy.

All health professions promulgate the idea that treatment should be based on pathogenesis. Psychiatric research evaluates treatment approaches for specific diagnoses. Education is then based on evidence of effectiveness of these approaches. Evidence of treatment efficacy exists for pharmacological, cognitive-behavioral, and psychodynamic approaches.[10,11,12] When we are caring for an individual patient, however, the right treatment does not just mean selecting from among types of therapy.[13] It means adjusting the therapeutic process to the understanding of the sources of the patient's pain. All mental health services are limited by frequent dropping out.[14] Mental health professionals might wonder to what extent this drop out reflects our inability to address issues that seem relevant to our patients. I submit that many patients will trust us when we frame their individual circumstances in terms of their aspiration to love and be loved.

The Ultimate Reason We Avoid Love

We have just had a prolonged excursion through the myriad ways that adults fail to establish and sustain a loving relationship. Do we have a legitimate expertise in love? Do we sufficiently understand its successes and failures? Are we able to rescue relationships from the jaws of defeat through our ability to recognize and repair mishandled moments? I think the answers to these questions are generally closer to "no" than to "yes." The mental health professions may avoid the emotionally evocative subject of love because we are unconfident in this arena. We lack assurance that we can think clearly about what love is and about how individuals interfere with their aspirations to live in harmony. Although people outside our professions may assume that we know this subject well, we recognize that they overestimate our mastery of the topic. We are a bit embarrassed by our settling for paradigms that fail to engage the vital processes of our lives. I am cautiously optimistic that we may be able to do a bit better in this regard.

References

1 Sondheim, S., & Wheeler, H. (1973). A little night music (music and lyrics). Musical Theater Production.
2 Harris, J. (2012). Lovesickness. Archives of General Psychiatry, 69(6), 549.
3 Brüne, M. (2003). Erotomanic stalking in evolutionary perspective. Behavioral Sciences & the Law, 21(1), 83–88.
4 Berscheid, E. (2006). Searching for the meaning of "love". In R.J. Sternberg & K. Weis, The new psychology of love (pp. 171–184). New Haven: Yale University Press.
5 Levine, S. (2006). Demystifying love: Plain talk for the mental health professional. New York: Routledge.
6 Bowlby, J. (1988). Developmental psychiatry comes of age. American Journal of Psychiatry, 145(1), 1–10.
7 Singer, I. (2009). Philosphy of love: A partial summing up. Cambridge, Massachusetts: The MIT Press.
8 Lewis, C.S. (1960). The four loves. London: Geoffrey Bles.
9 Carnes, P.J., & Adams, K.M. (2002) Clinical management of sexual addiction, New York: Brunner/Routledge.
10 Pigott, H.E., Leventhal, A.M., Alter, G.S., & Boren, J.J. (2010). Efficacy and effectiveness of antidepressants: Current status of research. Psychother Psychosom, 79(5), 267–279.
11 Farchione, T.J., Fairholme, C.P., Ellard, K.K., Boisseau, C.L., Thompson-Hollands, J., Carl, J.R., Gallagher, M.W., & Barlow, D.H. (2012). Unified protocol for transdiagnostic treatment of emotional disorders: a randomized controlled trial. Behavioral Therapy, 43(3), 666–678.

12 Busch, F.N., Milrod, B.L., Singer, M.B., & Aronson, A.C. (2011). *Manual of panic focused psychodynamic psychotherapy: Extended range.* London, UK: Routledge.
13 Kasdin, A.E. (2008). Evidence-based treatment and practice: New opportunities to bridge clinical research and practice, enhance our knowledge base, and improve patient care. *American Psychologist, 4,* 146–159.
14 Barrett, M.S., Chau, W., Crits-Christoph, P., Gibbons, B., & Thompson, D. (2008). Early withdrawal from mental health treatment: Implications for psychotherapy practice. *Psychotherapy Theory, Research, Practice, Training, 45*(2), 247–267.

3

LOVE PROBLEMS MANIFESTED
DURING COURTSHIP

Courtship is a crucial health process, a potential life-enhancing exploration of a new relationship with its psychological, social, sexual, familial, economic, and recreational possibilities. In various literatures, it is narrowly discussed through the widely celebrated falling in love process. Psychiatric discourses on falling in love focus on the imaginative excursions of individuals rather than the actual assessment processes between the individuals.[1] We clinicians do not hear much from our coupled patients about past courtship processes unless they question what, in retrospective, seems to have determined their poor judgment about their mate. Single patients teach us more about the evolution of courtship, particularly when they come upon a barrier, are emotionally injured, or experience destructive self-criticism, jealousy, or substance abuse. We also learn of courtship disappointments from our unattached patients who won't risk another disappointment. Even though we are not entirely in the dark about the private vetting processes of courtship,[2] their diverse pathologies make us realize how little we actually know about conscious and hidden aspects of becoming part of a new couple. Our reasonable sounding knowledge is largely speculative and biased towards the emphasis on early developmental processes rather than cognitive appraisal of both partners' circumstances and capacities.[3]

This chapter discusses the division of the compendium labeled *Impediments to Establishing a Loving Relationship* (Table 3.1). We are interested in the clinically apparent barriers to the establishment of a trusting, affectionate, dependable, stabilizing comfort with one another. When this mutual comfort is attained, the couple will likely consider their new subjective state as love. Such love, of course, usually includes sex. Readers should not be misled by the frequent discussions about sex in this chapter. The sexual issues are reflections of the obstacles preventing the establishment of the stabilizing enriching comfort of a loving attachment.

The Iconic Psychopathology

The "H-4" category in Table 3.1, "patterned loss of sexual interest in increasingly committed relationships," will be discussed first. The failure to feel both affection

Table 3.1 Impediments to Establishing a Loving Relationship

A. Major physical disabilities
B. Major cognitive disabilities
C. Major mental illness
D. Gender identity disorders
E. Character pathology
F. Select paraphilias
G. Lifelong sexual dysfunctions
H. Courtship disappointments
   1. Falling in love with the unreachable, unavailable, or those who are not even aware
   2. Rejection
   3. Refusal to commit to marriage
   4. Patterned loss of sexual interest in increasingly committed relationships

and sexual desire for the same person is a classic psychopathology that is typically manifested in courtship. This particular pattern is manifested after a gradual, initially pleasing, exciting process of learning about each other has occurred. While the affected person does not understand its source, what he or she knows is that after a pleasant process of psychological and physical intimacy with a highly valued person, sexual desire for the new partner dramatically diminishes. The avoidance of sex eventually becomes conspicuous to the partner. When the afflicted person attempts to have sex in order to deny the motivated avoidance, anxiety, panic, nausea, dizziness or headache, and sexual dysfunction appear. These symptoms of aversion are quite confusing because the person thinks that the partner is lovable, acceptable as a mate, and is physically attractive. The person knows that the idea of sex with another person, although morally problematic, is still enticing. The baffled partner ruminates about the answers to five questions about this new circumstance:

1. Am I not sufficiently physically attractive?
2. Am I not sufficiently intellectually attractive?
3. Am I a sexual disappointment?
4. Is there is someone else in the picture?
5. Is my partner homosexual?

The partner is not usually informed if the same phenomenon occurred during a previous courtship.

This psychopathology's major symptom pattern is manifested close to the moment when the person feels that *This is the one for me.* It often follows the public announcement of engagement, but it can also occur after marriage. To the best of my knowledge Sigmund Freud was the first physician to appreciate this situation. He saw it as a male problem. In his paper, On the Universal Tendency to Debasement in the Sphere of Love, in language that is so different from our own, he described this as the key to understanding *psychical impotence*.[4] I am charmed by what seems to be his sense of propriety, which is reflected in his unwillingness to employ penis, vagina, or sexual intercourse. He also assumed his audience was male. Others did not find it so quaint. Foucault wrote that it is a reflection of the cultural ambivalence to describe sexual life in its actual forms that gripped early 20th-century psychiatrists and led them to pathologize and distort the truth about the variety of sexual styles.[5]

> If the practicing psycho-analyst asks himself on account of what disorder people most often come to him for help, he is bound to reply—disregarding the many forms of anxiety—that it is psychical impotence. This singular disturbance affects men of strongly libidinous natures, and manifests itself in a refusal by the executive organs of sexuality to carry out the sex act, although before and after they may show themselves to be intact and capable of performing the act, and although a strong psychical inclination to carry it out is present. (Freud, 1912)

In the years since this article appeared, this psychopathology of love has been recognized to exist among sexual minority populations.[6] It is variously labeled love/lust split, the Madonna/Whore complex, psychological impotence, and Acquired Hypoactive Sexual Desire Disorder. Freud thought that its ultimate cause was an incestuous fixation on the mother or sister. He perceived that many symptomatic gradations of impotence shared this source. Although publishers packaged this and two related articles under contributions to the psychology of love, his theory more specifically purported to explain impotence. Fifteen years later his colleague convincingly argued that there were innumerable background factors and social contexts encountered among impotent men, not simply maternal incestuous fixation.[7] This broader-based idea was strongly supported in Masters and Johnson's clinical analysis.[8] They described a large array of background factors found among 213 couples in therapy. Only some of their cases were due to maternal dominance—a description that seems roughly compatible with Freud's etiological concept. The sex therapy field that was stimulated by Masters and Johnson's work unfortunately lost sight of the psychopathology of courtship in which a person cannot feel love and sexual desire for the same person.

Even though he overgeneralized the importance of one dynamic among impotent men, Freud gave the world a lovely image for sexual development. He posited that the sexual instinct (libido) consists of an affectionate and a sensual current that must be focused on the same person in order to have a fulfilling love relationship. These currents are ordinarily split apart, he posited, by Oedipal conflicts and often are not combined again until at least late adolescence. He thought sexual health and mature love required the two currents of libido to settle upon the same person, whom he referred to as the love object.

This notion seems to make the classic courtship psychopathology of love understandable. The man's aversion to his attractive, respect-worthy fiancée is caused by his unconscious link between her and his mother. Sex with his fiancée is akin to committing the heinous act of incest. For our purposes, his symptom of impotence with the fiancée is far less important than his aversion to having physical intimacy with her. He does not want to have sex with her. When this psychopathology affects a woman—and it frequently does—she, too, does not want to have sex with her otherwise beloved partner.

The title of Freud's 1912 paper highlights degradation. He suggested that men need to feel superior to their sexual partners in order to rid themselves of the incest taboo and realize their sexual pleasure potentials. This private sense of superiority is what was meant by intrapsychic degradation. When a man's executive organs of sexuality (sic) did not function with his fiancée or wife but did reliably with women he thought of as being of lesser status, the man could not accomplish what others do—that is, subtly think of their partners as inferior. Apparently, the fiancée is idealized and desexualized rather than privately degraded. Subsequent psychoanalysts have made clear that they regard love and aggression as inextricably related within the unconscious mind.[9,10] In some sense, patriarchy may accomplish this degradation for men who remain potent with their love objects.

Even in today's world, some cases presenting with a loss of sexual desire for a loved partner seem to be due to a strong unhealthy attachment to a parent. The sex tease song, "My Heart Belongs to Daddy," and the often-heard statement from impotent men raised alone by a never dating mother, "I'm my mother's entire world" conjure parental fixation. But the question needs to be asked, "What does parental fixation mean?" Does it include any parent-child problem that interferes with the uniting of the sensual and affectionate currents of libido? Does it only refer to failures to individuate from parents that have a residue of unconscious erotic fixation? If we include all varieties of parent-child relationship issues in the meaning of parental fixation, we can, at most, conclude that personal meanings of past parental relationships are likely to be germane to this psychopathology. If we arbitrarily define parental fixation as involving incestuous undertones, we can note the other pathways to the same dramatic loss of desire after the partner becomes "the one."

1. **Men and women who seem to have unconsciously turned their fiancés into the good parent that they never had.** The partner's love is needed to stabilize, comfort, and encourage them in the manner they had hoped their parent would have provided. They often feel resentment, derision, and disrespect for their parents and avoid them. They never want to be dependent on a person again because they recall the hurt stemming from their parent's failure to emotionally provide for them. Some individuals with this psychopathology have histories of being abandoned by a parent after divorce. Their sexual current may be confined to masturbation or they may be prone to affairs or Internet-based sexual excitements. They may seem to be perpetually adolescent in the sense that the libido can't alight on the love object.

2. **Prolonged devotion to sexual experiences with multiple partners in a quest for the excitement of the new.** These individuals may readily share

their previous seductive strategies with the clinician and comment that the hunt, rather than the actual sexual experiences, has been the central source of arousal. The relational context of the sexually receptive partner who also shares the ordinary complex multitasking of life with him or her is not exciting. Such men have been immortalized as varieties of Don Juan. Such women have been demeaned as promiscuous or caricatured as a Jezebel. Both comparisons seem to imply permanence of behavior rather than a more optimistic view as a phase of development as in sowing one's wild oats or reacting this way to a recent divorce.

3. **Prolonged adolescent dependence on pornographic and other commercial sexual outlets makes the transition to sexually loving a partner in the ordinary complex living context difficult.** It is as though sex with strangers or the images of the sexual behaviors of others is safe enough to be arousing; the reality of personal sex in a psychologically intimate context is more frightening. Many of these people dupe the fiancée with the explanation that they wanted to wait until marriage to have sexual intimacy out of partner respect or religious principles.

4. **After years of a pattern of sexual excesses involving commercial and noncommercial sexual relationships**—a prolonged period of sowing one's wild oats, without sexual dysfunction, the man's new loving partner becomes the source of sexual dread.

5. **The man with a fetish who does not realize its powerful role in enabling his potency with a partner or who does realize it but is too frightened to reveal this aspect of his life to his fiancée.** The fetish may take many forms but always poses the issue of revelation. His turmoil generates his loss of desire.

6. **An escape from acknowledgement of a homoerotic orientation.** This is the most culturally apparent source of the psychopathology. The person, formerly employing repression, suppression or deceit comes to be aware through their growing aversion for sex that he or she feels increasingly attracted to same sex persons or images.

I think of the failure to feel affection and sexual desire for the same person as an iconic psychopathology. Its power to defeat the aspiration to integrate an evolving satisfying sexual life with other important domains of the couple's life is impressive. It serves as a vital signpost for clinicians because it directs our search for its cause to the patient's development rather than the characteristics of the partner and their interactions. It is iconic in that it warns us to be psychoanalytic enough to think of the man or woman's individual development but not a zealous Freudian who would make the error of asserting a singular remote incestuous etiology. We must be prepared to work out the specific details of the pathogenesis patient by patient.

Regardless of which of the seven apparent pathways to this psychopathology of courtship the patient seems to have, the pattern ultimately forces the couple into dissolution or into an asexual companionate life together. In discussing the psychopathology with the couple, the clinician has to be sufficiently realistic, courageous, and ethical to help the couple to consider what it means for each of them if it cannot be ameliorated. We should not pretend this is an easy pattern to reverse. Treatment is ideally directed to the symptom bearer not the couple. The treatment approach that makes sense to me is a long-term one that focuses on the specific pathogenesis.

It is my impression that many mental health professionals, including sex and marital therapists, fail to perceive this situation among their patients with Hypoactive Sexual Desire Disorder. They ask the right question. What explains how a series of pleasurable relationship-building sexual acts became the source of dread and anxiety? But they look in the wrong direction for the answer. As a result, many patients drop out of treatment.

The lovely image of the two currents of libido breaking apart in early childhood, roaming around separately until psychosexual maturity allows them to recombine and focus on the loved person is only a metaphor. If it corresponds to the neural basis of the development of the brain's capacity to love, the metaphor brings us only to the opportunity healthy new couples have for happy sexual explorations with each other. This psychopathology prevents this enhancing process from occurring.

Permutations of Rejection—Categories H 1–3

When courtship works out well, both individuals have assessed the other's social, psychological, and economic assets and liabilities and found the whole person acceptable. They have passed each other's tests, however unsophisticated these may have been. Each has imagined a happy future together. When they confess their intense pleasure in each other's being, acknowledge that they love the other, and seem to want to be with one another all the time, they know that they are their beloved's beloved. Getting to this point, at whatever age, means that they survived their differing requirements for attaching to another person and managed to not see or to downplay the significance of what limitations that they did perceive. Optimism is inherent in this process. But there is always the question of the person's sensibilities.

Of course, I am not going to marry him! He is 71 years old and already has heart problems. We are enjoying our companionship. He takes me to the movies, plays, out to eat, and introduces me to new people. All this is wonderful after my years of being only with my women friends and family. Marriage is for the young. I want to be his friend, not his caretaker. This is a two-way street, you know. Why would anyone expect that he would want to be the caretaker of a 69-year-old woman when I have my own health problems? There is no good reason to talk about marriage; be realistic!

Love is not always blind but never-married people often have difficulty being realistic during courtship. Older people may have a far better grasp of the significance of social circumstances, and they have a better sense of how character traits observed in courtship play out over time. This advantage of age and previous painful experience is counterbalanced by fewer future opportunities for a sexually loving bond. Older courting persons typically consider social circumstances, character traits, and likelihood of subsequent opportunities in their vetting processes.

Character traits are the habitual patterns of behavior that persist from one developmental stage to another. People experience the traits of their partner, but they often don't seem to appreciate their long-term meaning. Consider these traits that are often evidenced in courtship: organized, disorganized, warm, unemotional, expressive, inscrutable, loves sexual behavior, tense during sex, healthy, chronically ill, generous, stingy, empathic, unaware, trusting, suspicious, socially avoidant, gregarious, interested in cooking, disinterested in food preparation, ambitious, unaspiring. As courting individuals discern whether they and the partner will be compatible over time, they are assessing such character traits.

Risk of disappointment is inherent in dating. Its potential for emotional damage begins when one person has a far more positive assessment of the partner than the partner has. Ken is happy enough to proceed with Susan but Ken is not everything that Susan wants and feels that she needs for her happiness. When their courtship ends, Ken is likely to have to cope with disappointment, dismay, self-doubt, and anger. He will wonder what the basis of this relationship failure was. Susan may be guilty, sad, concerned that she is too picky and worried about her future, but she has had agency enough to end it, which is a subtle source of pride. These ordinary casualties of courtship may induce temporary DSM-5 diagnoses of anxiety, mood, or substance abuse. But they are not all temporary. At some point, many people decide that they have had their last courtship disappointment and never make themselves available as a potential life partner again.

Falling in love invests the other person with great meaning, interest, and optimism. But when the other person's private conscious assessment concludes that the fit is not good enough, he or she is unable to provide a similar sustained investment of interest, pleasure, and optimism. The accurate discernment of the other person's regard is quite a challenge early in courtship. Individuals may decide, after the partner is deeply entrenched in them, that the partner was "just not the right one." This is a common form of the Ken and Susan story. But there are those who use the refrain of not having met the right one yet as a comforting rationalization for their fears of commitment stemming from family of origin issues. While it is a lovely project for a clinician when this is a patient's chief complaint, most of the time it is not the reason for requesting assistance. It is up to the clinician to expose the rationalization. It is a difficult clinical discernment to make because most couples do not fall in love at the same time at the same rate, and past relationships may not get much talk time in psychotherapy. We need to have this subtle courtship pathology in our minds in order to identify those who reject and flee rather than face their fears of attachment. We need to be willing to give the patient the benefit of the doubt that he or she is not completely aware of the motives for the recurrent rejection of partners.

We would like to assume that two people vet one another during courtship on a level playing field that allows love to blossom into commitment if each whole-heartedly accepts the other. This, however, is not always the case. The natural history of falling in love is not necessarily a lifetime commitment. There are those who never want to marry, don't believe in it, don't believe they are suited for it, don't want to ever do it again, or are not ready to settle down. Some believe only in serial monogamy for as long as the intense pleasure of the relationship lasts. When such attitudes are clearly stated from the onset and repeated as the courtship evolves, their relationship has to absorb this belief system. When they are not revealed, however, the unsuspecting partner who assumes that their mutual pleasure in each other's company naturally would lead to permanence may be deeply wounded. If the truth were to be known, the rejecting partner would be accused of insincerity, dishonesty, or narcissism because he or she was motivated to facilitate falling in love because *What is better than new love?* The person only begins to withdraw when the other is insistent upon a commitment. While many individuals who are averse to marriage find resolution in long-term cohabitation without a marriage—a pattern well modeled in sexual minority communities—this dynamic destroys many would be couples. The mental health professional is more apt to see the one who was inexplicably abandoned when the relationship seemed to be going well than the one who hurt yet another person.

During courtship, people do not reveal to their partner that they are consciously weighing and measuring everything about the other. That would be impolite and dangerous. Clinicians may expect some anxiety about the partner considering the importance of choosing the right mate. These worries, if shared with anyone, tend to be communicated to friends or family. Courtship can generate an anxiety disorder when emotions, meanings, and problematic behaviors from previous courtships or parental attachments augment these worries. The person's new symptoms may overwhelm a friend, but a clinician who grasps that courtship is stirring up remote issues can be remarkably useful.

Another pathway to courtship pathology seems to come from inattention to the vetting process. Some complain that they fall in love too easily, too often. It is as though being paid attention to, being the center of another's life, being the object of social or sexual desire are sufficient to initiate the act of imagination that stimulates the affective excitement of a new relationship. The character traits or social circumstances of new person are far less important than the interest offered. Even the patient recognizes that there must be something in them that makes them desperate to love and be loved. When looking back, they may conclude that they were not very discriminating. This is an invitation to the clinician to define that something within them and to discuss it in a supportive, optimistic fashion.

In the year since a 59-year-old married father of three grown children announced his homosexual orientation and divorced, he has fallen in love with four men and has had a friends-with-benefits relationship with two others. He was devastated after his new love of six weeks told him that he had lost his feelings for him and no longer wanted to see him. Returning to therapy in a crisis of anxiety, insomnia, and lack of concentration, he reported that when his new gay friends told him that he could do better, he felt briefly better. But, the man who looked so much like his father and was so pleased to be with him was a world apart in education, interests, and economic strata. The patient asked me why he fell in love like a moonstruck adolescent. I smiled. You are relatively inexperienced in the world of men. Perhaps you are like an older teenager exploring love/sex in the gay community. He laughed, then cried and said that he is terribly afraid of being alone.

Then there are those patterns of becoming attached to unreachable, unavailable, or unlikely persons. This is often the chief reason for seeking psychiatric care. The patient sees the pattern, can't understand its presence, and can't break off the relationship. The patient feels as if there is no cure for their unilateral fascination with the new unsuitable love object. The psychotherapist is often eager to generate answers to what lies behind this maladaptive courtship pattern based on the patient's unique life history. He or she is prepared to patiently explore the meanings of the love object and the motives for the pursuit through the usual tools of associations to previous relationships, defenses against emotional authenticity and specific sexual interests. The trouble often is that the patient's sincerity about wanting the answers is often exceeded by the patient's fear of the answers or at least fear of the answers being known by the therapist.

A 40-year-old divorced woman began to tell me the story of her recent uneasy three-month courtship. Months after her divorce was final, she fell in love from afar with a fellow graduate student, a Roman Catholic priest. She pursued him. After their relationship had its third episode of minor sexual intimacy, without discussing it further, he made it difficult to be alone together. He pretended not to see her continuing warm offers of socialization as anything more than friendship until she moved on.

With me, she wondered what had motivated her ardor towards him. Did I really think it was possible for this kind man to relinquish his values and vows for me? I am not even Catholic! What would I have done if he did? Was I toying with him? Was this my lark, my distraction from my situation? Did I really think he would become a stepfather for my girls? Was I crazy? We agreed to explore these questions. She cancelled her next appointment with the promise to call back in a week. She never did.

I have also been defeated in my attempt to understand such relationships by patients who maintain their relationship with me but are so busy with other responsibilities that their infrequent visits leave no possibility to sustain the investigation. Such situations remind me that the conduct of one's courtships—their motives for the choice of partner, the life history revealed, and the attitudes displayed to the partner—are deeply personal matters that are difficult to reveal to anyone. The wish to discuss the topic coexists with the wish not to discuss it.

Even when this dialect tension is gradually overcome, however, there is another obstacle to understanding the processes of courtship—capturing the interactive process between two people is far too difficult for most of us to describe. I suspect that this explains why so much of the psychiatric literature about courtship barriers is so heavily focused on the patient's developmental meanings rather than the patient's actual interactions with the partner. It also explains our gratitude to novelists who allow us to experience the circumstances of courtship of their protagonist, enabling us to see elements of ourselves in their characters' lives.

Another way psychotherapists can glimpse the processes of courtship and the internal processes of early love is through erotic transference. Patients may fall in love with us quickly or slowly (or not at all). Although we quickly technically label the phenomenon as transference love, its emotional intensity and preoccupying nature feels to the patient like real, genuine, transforming romantic love. The clinician, bounded by a reality that dictates no consummation, is challenged to be respectful, to illuminate the patient's longings for a rich interpersonal sexual relationship, and to link elements of the past to the current affective state. When a patient and therapist can deal with the erotic transference well, their bond increases in trust, respect, and mutual grasp of the ordinary complexity of intimate relationships. It is actually a thing of beauty to deal respectfully with the patient's ardor and have it translate into better functioning in the world.[11]

Sexual Disorders That are Pathologies of Courtship

Table 3.1 contains three sexual disorder categories: gender identity disorders (known as Gender Dysphoria in DSM-5), select paraphilias, and lifelong sexual dysfunctions. These well known patterns generate impediments to courtship along a spectrum of severity. When severe, they preclude courtship by their intense preoccupation with their gender sense, or through socially off-putting behaviors, including criminal means of sexual arousal or overwhelming anxiety about partner sexual interaction. As a result, no courtship gets underway. However, among individuals with paraphilia or sexual dysfunction, sex without a relationship or commercial sex may occur. While these individuals may aspire to courtship to end their loneliness, their clumsy efforts to initiate dating are typically ineffective. Clinicians might at times reconsider their problems as impediments to courtship rather than highlight their psychiatric disorder as something to directly cure.

On the other end of the spectrum, the courtship impediments posed by these three sexual categories profoundly restrict the pool of potential partners. People who are upfront about their gender struggles can elicit sympathy for their mental

31

anguish and support from friends for their plans to transition, but this does not readily translate into a sensual process. The person may have grave doubts about what he or she will feel and express during sex. The potential partner, knowing of the person's gender sense, may be hesitant, confused, and anxious at the prospect of having sex with someone with a dramatic gender mosaic despite the sexual attraction that may have been stimulated by their psychological intimacy. It is a big leap from friend to lover. On the other hand, there are those who seem to be particularly interested in sex with those with conspicuous gender identity mosaics. Unfortunately, clinicians hear about this primarily in terms of those who want to have sex with such a person rather than want to enter into a lasting relationship with them. These gender patients tend to become commodities in the minds of those who tell us about their fascination or addiction to such male-female mosaic persons.

In contrast, men whose sexual patterns are voyeurism, exhibitionism, and pedophilia do not offer much sexually to partners. While men with these patterns occasionally court and marry, they may do so without sexual expression during courtship. Marriage, per se, with its presumed ready access to partner genital sex, does not seem to change the fixed paraphilic need to surreptitiously look upon, exhibit to, and shock unsuspecting young adolescents, or to pursue the grooming of underage partners. Most of these people are perceived to have poor social skills. Here is an exception.

A handsome well spoken mid-30s salesman has been fascinated with urine flowing from women's bodies since he was in a public toilet stall with his grandmother thirty years ago. Never married, he has had a series of girlfriends since college. He occasionally has had intercourse but typically could not ejaculate even by thinking of one of his favorite images: water squirting from a pipe coming out of a hillside. Each partner has found it weird that before or after sex he asks to watch her urinate. I met him after he was arrested for placing a camera in a women's public bathroom.

Lifelong sexual dysfunctions pose significant challenges to courtship because most partners value sexual opportunity and the partner's enjoyment of sex. The least destructive to courtship is female anorgasmia. The woman can enjoy sex despite the failure to attain orgasm by manual, oral, or intercourse stimulation. Optimism may still prevail in her and her partner about the future if she is in her twenties or early thirties. She has little reason to avoid sex during courtship. An older anorgasmic woman may convince her partner that she does not mind her lack of orgasm and that she loves to please him or her. Some partners, however, may find this pattern a strong negative factor when considering the woman's suitability as a long-term partner.

Unfortunately for women and men with aversions or arousal disorders and for women with intense dyspareunia or vaginismus, the situation is not as positive.

Not only are partners suspicious of the meaning of these patterns for the future, the symptom bearer is frightened and avoidant of sexual opportunity.

A 48-year-old divorcing woman had never consummated her 24-year marriage because of vaginismus. When she began dating, she broke off two pleasant new relationships because she thought sexual intercourse was soon expected. Her 20-years-her-senior third partner was happy with her because of his intractable erectile dysfunction. She presented herself as sympathetic and not demanding. He shattered her happiness and induced panic when he expressed a fervent wish to enter her vagina with his fingers and a vibrator. Previously unwilling to invest herself in a process of trying to overcome her lifelong problem, she came seeking advice on how to tell him no. She was too embarrassed to tell him the truth.

While the compendium lists the three sexual disorders as courtship impediments, these disorders often coexist in the same person. In whatever combination they present, however, it is useful to recognize that they severely limit the potential mate pool.

A thirty-year-old androgynous male, who aspires to live as a woman, has had limited partner sexual involvement. During his only sexual intercourse experience with a woman, he switched genitalia in his imagination: his penis was her penis and her vagina was his vagina. He did not ejaculate. He declined the opportunity to repeat the experience. He masturbates to orgasm several times per week. After several years, he acquired a second sexual partner, a pre-surgical transsexual biological male. After he confessed his lifelong fantasy of being bound and subdued for sex, they had many sexual experiences in which either his arms or all limbs were tied and he was stimulated manually and orally. Although he typically could not ejaculate, he was clear that trusting surrender to the wishes of the other was exciting because for him it represented being a woman. Being an avid reader of transsexual fiction, he recognized that his submission fantasies are not unusual. "I have no interest in being the dominant. I want to be bound and held tightly."

Character Pathology

The diagnosis of character disorder is a professional synthesis that takes into account behaviors manifested in different contexts. Among ourselves, we speak of character pathology as though it is a generally accepted version of reality. We should occasionally remind ourselves that while the patients whom we think of as having narcissistic, borderline, sociopathic, avoidant, paranoid, obsessive-compulsive, schizoid, or mixed character disorders court, their dates are only assessing their behaviors. Partners are not expected to make the same synthesis that professionals do. Nonetheless, partners are experiencing the character disorder in action. The functional meaning of character disorders is that they impede courtship in one of four ways.

1. A central feature of the personality—self-centeredness, inconstancy, uncaring hurtfulness to others, hesitation to try new things, argumentativeness, or affective flatness—may make individuals unappealing to discerning others.
2. They are limited in their capacity to create a trusting, emotionally authentic sharing of the self with the other. When others speak of their requirements for happiness, such as having a partner who is interested in their inner life, one who is behaviorally reliable, one who remains within the law and treats others fairly, one who is socially engaged with others, or one who is emotionally responsive or who has conventional aspirations of closeness to family and friends, the character disordered person may quickly lose interest.
3. Their episodic expressions of anger, criticisms, or disappointment may be too intense for the circumstances and frighten away the partner.
4. They tend to see their courtship problems as located in the partner's deficiencies and style and have a difficult time compromising because they take little personal responsibility for the circumstance.

While these disadvantages impede courtship for some character-disordered patients, many of these individuals find new love because they also have appealing features. These traits may be kindness, intelligence, athleticism, wealth, musical talent, love for animals, beauty, etc. But they also may be an integral part of the character pathology. The confidence of the narcissistic, the sexual excitement of the borderline, the daring of the sociopath, the quiet pleasures of the avoidant, the perceptiveness of the paranoid, and the stability of the obsessive-compulsive come to mind. It is just that over time in the courtship these same traits begin to appear in a new light.

Highly perceptive people may spot an incompatible trait upon first exposure. Less perceptive, intuitive people may recoil without knowing why. Others require more time to discern their fundamental incompatibility with the man or woman whose behavioral style recurrently causes problems. If they aren't figured out during courtship, these behaviors limit the potential of the couple to realize the fullness of love's potential.

I have found that it is useful to many character-disordered people to have their frustration in courtship explained to them as a problematic trait that limits their lovability. In dealing with a narcissistic person, for instance, he or she may appreciate being taught that courtship is a two-way process. Interest in and consideration of the other is a requirement and putting the needs of the partner first needs to occur at a reasonable rate. Many patients are grateful for the incisive behavioral translation of the diagnosis. Sharing the diagnostic label is not nearly as important as translating the traits into new behavioral goals.

There seems to be a great deal of truth in the adage that there is someone for everyone in the universe. Given the personality style of the patient, without an effort to improve one's behavior in the direction of interest in and respect for the individuality of the partner, the patient needs to know that the person who may be found in the future may have too many limitations to be ultimately pleasing. Martin Buber's concept of I-Thou relationships helps many people with character pathology grasp the goal. A narcissist emphasizes I too much and insufficiently invests in Thou. The paranoid person is challenged to develop trust in Thou. The clinician has to find a way to explain the problem so that it is both understood and provides a roadmap to more successful courtships.

Conspicuous Disabilities—Categories A–C

Certain individuals face major courtship limitations based on their physical or psychiatric illnesses. Persons with significant congenital orthopedic deformities, paraplegia, recently treated breast cancer in remission, post-traumatic stress disorder with cognitive impairment from a war injury, schizophrenia, or alcoholism, for instance, are often hopeless about finding a mate. Not only do they have self-concepts that reverberate around *Who would want me*, others deem them a poor risk for partnership. Clinicians should act like they understand the two sides of this coin. The limited pool of available partners for the physically and mentally limited is part of the inherent disadvantage of the disability. Over time, this arduous reality may become a significant source of unhappiness, loneliness, and sexual frustration. As these emotional forces well up, the psychiatric patient's depression may be viewed as an exacerbation of the schizophrenia, bipolar disorder, PTSD, or substance abuse rather than a reaction to the frustration in courtship. The mental health professional needs to be able to discuss the sources of suffering among the physically and mentally impaired so as to be helpful within the limitations posed by the disability.

A woman in her twenties, after her second psychotic break, spent seven years with intermittent suicidal preoccupations and made three suicide attempts. She often expressed her despair over her frustrated aspiration to marry and to be a mother. During this time, she ran from the few males who expressed interest in her. At age 37 she married a gentle nervous man who was the noncustodial parent of a twelve-year-old daughter. Today, 30 years later, they remain married. Their lives are limited by her schizophrenia and his passivity and rigidity. Periodically, she laments the past two decades without sexual behavior and is angry at his preference for pornography, but she returns to her gratitude towards this unambitious man for staying with her. Despite their recurrent travails, the couple has managed major life events reasonably well with a few exacerbations of her psychosis. His consistent insistence that he loves her, even when she is psychotically decompensated, enables her to believe him.

From her first psychotic break at age 17 until her marriage 20 years later, the courtship barrier seemed insurmountable. I was delighted to learn that I had been wrong. She credits the therapist who calmly accepted her love and her fear that she would spend her life alone for her ability years later to trust that another man might find her to be a good person to love. When first hospitalized, she believed that she smelled so badly that no one would want to be near her. Although her hygiene was fastidious, her delusion that people moved away from her when in public led to her diagnosis of schizophrenia. If such a person appeared in my practice today, I hope I would be able to more quickly attend to both her psychotic illness and its devastating effects on her aspiration to find a man to love and to be loved by. Never a mother, she enjoys being a grandmother in part because she never thought such a joyful relationship would be possible for her.

References

1 Person, E. (1988). Falling in love. In E. Person, *Dreams of love and fateful encounters: The power of romantic passion* (pp. 29–49). New York: WW Norton.
2 Myers, L. (2010). Single again. In S.B. Levine, C.B. Risen, & S.E. Althof, *Handbook of clinical sexuality for mental health professionals* (2nd ed., pp. 12–139). New York: Routledge.
3 Kernberg, O. (2012). *The inseparable nature of love and aggression: Clinical and theoretical perspectives*. Washington, DC: American Psychiatric Publishing.
4 Freud, S. (1912). On the universal tendency to debasement in the sphere of love. In S. Freud, *The standard edition of the complete psychological works of Sigmund Freud* (Vol. XI, pp. 177–190). London, England: Hogarth Press.
5 Foucault, M. (1978). Scientia sexualis. In M. Foucault, *The history of sexuality: Volume I an introduction* (pp. 51–74). New York: Pantheon Books.
6 Morin, J. (1995). *The erotic mind: Unlocking the inner sources of sexual passion and fulfillment*. New York: Harper Perennial.
7 Stekel, W.B. (1927). *Impotence in the male: The psychic disorders of sexual function in the male*. London: Boni and Liveright.
8 Masters, W.M., & Johnson, V. (1970). *Human sexual inadequacy*. Boston: Little Brown.
9 Gabbard, G.O. (1996). *Love and hate in the analystic setting*. Northvale, N.J.: Jason Aronson.
10 Kernberg, O.F. (2012). The inseparable nature of love and aggression: Clinical and theoretical perspectives. Washington, DC: American Psychiatric Press.
11 Levine, S.B. (1992). *Erotic feelings in therapy in sexual life: A clinician's guide*. (Chapter 15, pp. 216–230). New York: Plenum Publications.

4

IMPEDIMENTS THAT DIMINISH
A PERSON'S LOVABILITY

As we consider the subtle, often intangible forces that undermine a partner's ability to remain wholeheartedly invested in a relationship, we must recognize two inherent artifacts of the discussion. Relationships are by nature rapidly interactive. Person A behaves, person B reacts, and instantly, A reacts to B's reaction, etc. In this chapter, we will think about the forces that erode lovability as though they emanate solely from person A, the index person. Clinicians know of course, that the partner interprets A's behavior and gives it a meaning that may diminish or maximize its negative impact. While we will focus on person A's behavior as the stimulus, the behavior is really a surrogate for the meaning that the partner attributes to the behavior. While we attribute the behavior to A, the reaction to it belongs to B. Even this is an oversimplification, however, since A then reacts to B's tone and words. These two complexities—rapid reactivity to one another and meaning making—begin to explain why discussions of relationships are fraught with uncertainty. We oversimplify to assist us in understanding of how partners become emotionally and sexually withdrawn from their mates. But we realize that relationships are more complex than our explanations of them.

The love that tends to be dramatized in stories, lauded in song, extolled in poetry, represented in dance, and described in biographies tends to be new love, regardless if it is occurring in the young or older persons. The private psychological processes that we are considering here are infrequently the subjects of multidimensional cultural discourse.[1] Our topic is how relationship disappointment, dilemma, and anguish come about. It is the stuff of marital or individual therapy and well-rendered fiction. It is also a source of psychiatric illness, although, as pointed out in Chapter One, mental health professionals are hesitant to assert this.

Significance

Culture's hope for love is that it will deepen over time, become more nuanced and complex, and will remain pleasing even as a much clearer picture of the strengths and limitations of the partners emerge. With mutual understanding and acceptance, the partners become more psychologically intertwined with time. Their relationship health depends upon their discovering an acceptable balance between their oneness as a couple and their separateness as individuals.[2] A couple that has long been together is, therefore, simultaneously one and two. It might seem that I am describing healthy mature love except for the fact that young couples can have a comfortable oneness while being respectful of their psychological separateness. It might also appear that I am labeling evolving companionate love except for the fact that the deepening of love does not necessarily diminish the couple's mutual pleasure in their sexual behavior. Our question is less what to name love that continues to be mutually satisfying and appreciated as it evolves and more what happens to create disappointed, unsatisfying, resentful love. If we can assume that love has a potential trajectory of subtle satisfying growth over decades, we can appreciate that its impediments can temporarily slow or stop its growth, create a permanently lower set of the expectations, increase the sense of separateness, or completely dissolve the commitment to remain an entity.

The Sense of Violation

Clinicians sometimes speak of the marriage contract. The utility of this metaphor is that it clarifies relationship distress.[3] The contract contains three forms of obligations: 1. Those that have been explicitly agreed upon; 2. Private expectations that were never discussed; and 3. Unconscious assumptions about how the partner ought to behave. Many complaints about relationships convey the feeling that a previously made agreement was violated. Any violation by person A, whether delivered through words, behaviors, or lack of behavior, can instantly cause distress in a partner. Table 4.1 asks the reader to consider the possible meanings of behaviors and events for the partner. Meanings are always associated with affects, which may be so sudden and intense as to obscure the underlying meaning. Even when affects are not intense, meanings and their unconscious associations may not be quickly apparent. They may emerge only gradually as the person contemplates what has occurred. Whether we prefer to think of its categories as violations of a contract or impediments to loving, the items in Table 4.1 compile the diverse pathways to becoming less lovable to the partner. The compilation is by no means complete.

Table 4.1 Impediments That Diminish a Person's Lovability

A. Incompatible Sexual Identity Variations
B. Acquired Sexual Dysfunctions
C. Sexual Excess Patterns
D. Paraphilias
E. Character Traits That Alienate
F. Aggressive Behaviors
G. New Major Mental or Physical Illness
H. Other Sources of the Loss of Love
    a. Within Family Behavioral Patterns
    b. Criminality
    c. Infidelity

Incompatible Sexual Identity Variations

Individuals become a couple assuming that their sexual identities are compatible. Most people equate sexual identity with a gay, straight, or bisexual sexual orientation. They are unaware that it has two additional components that could impede their loving: gender identity and intention. It is a formidable challenge to a harmonious bond to absorb the news that the partner is now struggling with attraction to members, or a particular member, of the same sex. It stimulates hopelessness in the partner to have to compete for sexual interest with a person of opposite sex. The situation quickly becomes more complicated when questions begin to be raised. "Did you know about your orientation before?" "How could you not have known in adolescence and young adulthood?" "Why did you not tell me during courtship?" "What do you want to do?" "What do you want me to do now?" "Why is this occurring now?" "Is it because you are disappointed in me?" These questions, regardless of their answers, typically create profound resentment. This new situation feels like a betrayal of their contract.

Four years into a lesbian union, two years after successful artificial insemination, a woman tells her partner that she is interested in a man!

Twenty-five years into marriage, for the first time, a man confirms his wife's growing suspicion that he is gay. Six months previously, he became preoccupied with gay Internet sites. Two months previously, he had a wonderful evening of mutual revelation and sex with another married man he had chatted with over the Internet.

The underlying threat of the emerging awareness of an alternative orientation is abandonment. This outcome is not inevitable, however. Some couples seem to be able to survive these conditions, at least for a while, by employing a new arrangement. Some couples develop "an understanding" or "a night out policy" that accommodates the new desires of the mate. The announcement may lead others to employ three-person sexual experiences. Other couples have a tearful dialogue about it, make promises, and never discuss it further. Affairs begin or continue without future reference to it.

Our interest is in the impact of such announcements on the partner. The new information generally limits one's sense of safety about the future. "If not now, when will I be abandoned?" The partner may lose sexual interest because the announcement means that the mate does not have any genuine interest. "I don't want to have sex with someone who does not want me." Conversely, there may be a brief reclaiming operation during which the couple briefly intensifies their sexual behavior together. Whatever happens, however, partners begin thinking about their future elsewhere. Among individuals with children who divorce because of homosexuality, the ideal aftermath is cooperative coparenting, a supportive friendship that enables the ex-spouses to share family events in each other's company, the ability to care for one another during illness, and the continuing acknowledgement that they love each other still. The anger over abandonment and the differences between the promise and the delivery often subvert these seemingly ideal results.

For some, newly emerging homosexual desire is just one of many things subsumed under "for better or for worse."

A very religious 12-year-old had been enticed into sexual behavior with his 16-year-old brother episodically for two years. Thirty-five years later, a father of five, he began having strong homosexual desires and had sex with several male strangers. Intense anxiety led him to two brief courses of psychotherapy, which along with the substance abuse crises of their children, enabled him to focus on other matters. He and his wife have lived together happily, with occasional sex, since. She, also a deeply religious person, sees the problem as the unfortunate consequence of his family's rampant alcoholism. "He is not really gay, he is a traumatized person," she concluded. She is currently in treatment for depression and anxiety, which focuses on the continuing worries about the young adult children and their offspring. Prayer and forgiveness are integral aspects of their lives as individuals, as a couple and as an extended family.

Situations are also poignant when the emerging sexual identity issue is the wish to express one's self in a new gender. This has three typical forms: the married man who has secretly cross-dressed since adolescence; a masculine lesbian in a committed relationship with a woman; a coupled feminine homosexual man who decides to transition as a woman. Because transitioning is such an all-consuming preoccupation aimed at acquiring a new level of comfort in the world, the partner is presented with an ultimatum: "Either support me lovingly in my journey or let me do it on my own without you." The partner's immediate and subsequent reactions do not seem to be of much consequence to the intensely self-preoccupied transitioning person.[4] It is more, "How do I look in my makeup? and less, "How is it for you when I feminize?" The partner originally fell in love with a man or a woman; the new person is contrary to his or her orientation, so it is experienced as weirdly unnatural. It is usually infuriating that the transitioning person seems to consistently have little regard for what this means for the partner and the children.[4] The self-centeredness of the transitioning person is antithetical to a central idea about loving: sustainable love is a two-way process of putting one's needs second to the partner's needs. Far, far too much "I" and not enough "we" is destructive to the partner's ability to invest in the relationship. The partner's understanding, compassion, and sacrifice have limits that are lowered by the continuation of the narcissistic behaviors. On rare occasion, I have witnessed couples that absorb this transition, stay together, and live out their lives for the most part as two women.[5]

The emerging shifts of orientation or gender identity eventually create a publicly visible explanation for relationship change or loss. These contrast with newly announced sexual intentions. Ordinary sexual intentions involve giving and receiving sexual pleasures in a nonaggressive mutual fashion. When paraphilic strivings become apparent after several years of conventional sex, the ensuing dilemma often remains only known by the couple. Here are a few examples:

> A wife discovers that her husband has been spending money at a dominatrix's dungeon.
>
> A husband now wants to spank his wife, pull her hair to the point of pain and pretend that she is a sexually promiscuous woman that he has picked up at a bar. He no longer can ejaculate in her presence without some of these elements.
>
> A married man pressures his wife to have sex with another man while he watches.
>
> A husband pressures his wife to allow him to stimulate her anus with his tongue.

Before the paraphilic desires became insistently expressed, the partner intuitively valued the nurturing reassurance of the sense of oneness that their conventional sexual behaviors provided. Because paraphilias likely take their form from the man's eroticization of his unique anxiety provoking experiences, the partner cannot share the intense arousal that he gets from their reenactments. Once the paraphilic themes are introduced, sex induces the partner's awareness of their separateness. This lessens the bond to him. The partner may stay with him but the pleasure of sex diminishes when she (or he) has to play a role that is merely compliant with his needs.

These three sexual identity issues, although they differ in kind, create the same existential question for the partner: "What about me?" The partner often concludes, "I am not as important as I thought I was to my mate." This is not a circumstance that encourages pleasure, safety, trust, and optimism, although it may provoke compassion for the painful sources of the paraphilic development. The partner begins thinking of how to develop a new life elsewhere.

When some of these partners seek mental health services for the resultant new high levels of anxiety or depression, they may be too embarrassed to initially tell the clinician about the underlying sexual identity issue in their lives. They are relieved to be asked about it, however.

Acquired Sexual Dysfunctions

Clinicians tend to assume that coupled individuals expect that they will have a sexual life together that will be characterized by mutual desire, ease of arousal, and pain-free orgasmic experiences. Our nosology provides diagnoses for those who complain of deficiencies in one or more of these components in their individual or partnered lives. In research and many clinical settings, we encounter individuals whose sexual experiences do not live up to this assumption. They do not choose to undertake any medical or psychiatric effort to change their sexual lives. They seem not to be distressed about what exists. But among those who share the assumption and who used to have a sexual life without problems, the loss of desire, arousal, or orgasm can create a sense of deprivation. Often, the dysfunction is discussed by the partners with rancor and defensiveness or tensely avoided. If the problem is not resolved, the couple's sexual life together becomes less frequent, more one-sided, and fails to provide the assurance that one is loved. Their previously mutually enjoyable functional sex provided a wordless affirmation of being loved that only now, in their deprivation, do they clearly recognize.

While treatment focuses on the specific sexual dysfunction, it is actually the meaning of the pattern to the partner that determines much of the motivation for seeking that assistance. Any new sexual dysfunction—for instance, sexual aversion on the part of a mother of two children—can be a crisis or just a change, depending solely on the meaning of the sexual pattern to the partner. For some, the loss of her interest is an affront, a symptom of a problem between them or within her, a harbinger of a future without sex, a justification for extra-dyadic sex, an intolerable deprivation, or a normal reaction to caring for an infant. Sexual behavior is infused with much meaning, but some of these meanings only become apparent when dysfunction arrives.

When discussing women's sexual lives, clinicians usually use menopause as the great divide. The bias is that while menstruation is part of life, dysfunctions are generally psychosocial in origin, but after menopause, there are organically-based physiological forces at work. Of course, young women can and do have organic contributions to their dysfunctions and psychosocial influences can create acquired dysfunctions among menopausal women. These departures from an entire life of sexual functionality always have meanings to women and their partners. Occasionally these meanings coincide; often they do not.

When discussing men's sexual lives, the focus, however professionally disguised, is on his ability to get the job done. The *job* is to remain erect until a well-timed ejaculation occurs. When a man consistently fails in this role for an extended period of time, the partner often runs through a set of anxious meanings: he does not find me attractive, he does not like me, there is someone else, he has a hidden orientation, he is not much of a man, this is not fun, how long can I be supportive without showing my anger, how do I get him to professional help, etc. Warm, supportive encouragement, patience that comes from awareness of the ordinary vagaries of sexual function, and guidance to behave sexually in ways that are not dependent on the erection are ideal partner responses, but these cannot be expected to last forever.

In either gender, eventually the meaning of the established new dysfunction, particularly if the partner refuses to get assistance or if professional help disappoints, means that deprivation of the pleasures of sex will continue. Since sex is a nurturing process for both partners, functional sex wordlessly assures a husband or wife of masculine or feminine adequacy, attractiveness, acceptability, and a good-enough bond to the mate as well as erases minor resentments that grew up between sexual opportunities. Satisfying sex prevents the discomfort of longing for a new partner.

A new established sexual dysfunction lessens the pleasures of couplehood. It begs for explanation. The partner will provide it in his or her own mind regardless of its accuracy. Acquired sexual dysfunction often limits the sensations that are interpreted as love. It may significantly add to the forces of dissatisfaction already contained within the relationship.

Sexual excess patterns, which are discussed next, are often preceded by unexplained male sexual dysfunctions. Although these typically involve limited sexual desire, unreliable potency, and early ejaculation or anorgasmia in various combinations, many of them display the iconic psychopathology discussed in Chapter Three.

Sexual Excess Patterns

These have been long known in the culture as sexual addictions and more recently within the mental health professions as Hypersexual Disorder. These combinations of heavy reliance on masturbation, commercial sex, pornography, extramarital relationships, and Internet sexual socialization or cybersex games, when discovered, create a maelstrom of anger, anxiety, aversion, paranoia, despair, and exhaustion in the partner. In many, but not all, of these circumstances, the discovery of the sexual excess is the last straw. The man had already long burdened his partner with previous maladaptive behaviors that clinicians might label as mood disorders, anxiety disorders, addiction proneness, and attention deficit disorders. When some sexual excess patterns are effectively dealt with after their discovery, the sick role afforded to the person in treatment mitigates the risk of immediate, but not future, termination of the relationship.

Discovery of these patterns rearranges the partner. It reshapes her self-perceptions and her attitudes, as well as her behaviors toward him. The more she thinks about what she now knows about her mate's outside sexual activities, the more she feels that she is a foolish, dependent person for staying with someone who prefers commercial sexual gratification. She loses self-confidence and self-respect. She suddenly fears for her physical health and seeks reassurance that she does not have a sexually transmitted disease. The medical testing is the source of worry, rage, and humiliation. She feels that the emotional bond that enabled her to give herself sexually to him is over. Staying with him is now for financial support, the children's benefit, or to see if he can substantially change this behavior. Divorce becomes a preoccupation, even if it never is initiated. Partners are often so dismayed about their discoveries that hatred suffuses their beings. Divorce or relationship breakup is a frequent long-term outcome.

> A woman's suspicions about her husband's whereabouts and activities persisted for years after he returned to fidelity. She sought help four years later with the accurate description, "I've become paranoid."
>
> A woman, always a bit eccentric, became chronically hypomanic after learning about the extent of her husband's activities at strip clubs where he routinely entertained business associates.

A previously reasonably happily married woman who had long ago accepted her husband's low level of desire with equanimity, left home in a confused, depressed rage that lasted for months after discovering his credit card charges at a strip club and an expensive gift given to his new stripper friend.

Paraphilia

A minority of sexual excess situations are driven by a paraphilia. Paraphilia can be a significant source of the loss of lovability even without sexual excess, as noted previously. A liberal partner may initially think that everyone has a bit of kinkiness in them when she or he learns of a man's overvaluation of a body part, a fetish object, sadistic or masochistic fantasies or behaviors, cross-dressing for sex, or the man's wish to talk "dirty" about pedophilic or female promiscuity or rape. The partner may view it as a way of having a sexual adventure, an escape from the ordinariness of vanilla sex. Its persistence and insistence, however, soon teaches the partner that this is more than an evanescent exploratory game; it is a requirement for arousal and for the motivation to participate in sex. The partner realizes that she or he cannot match the degree of arousal that the unique favored scenario induces in the mate. Sex and its opportunities for its reassuring bonding function often disappear.

Character Traits that Alienate

This category may be the most important one in the compendium. It is quite a subtle matter, however. Character traits may be the common denominator that explains much of courtship success and failure and relationship quality. Character traits are discerned intuitively as familiar patterns of responses to diverse environments. These patterns have great private significance to the partners. Many happy people speak of their mates as a "good person." Their analysis of the other's fundamental nature concludes that he or she is appealingly positive—kind, compassionate, ambitious, competitive, religious, conservative, careful, child-centered, honest, generous, bright, etc. Many others speak of their partners as a "good fit." The partner may be like them in some important way—fun loving, accomplished, athletic, good looking, drug using, etc. The partner may have a trait that the person wishes to have for him or herself—good with money, accomplished, athletic, well-organized, tough, funny, self-confident, etc. The partner may also be experienced as a good fit because his or her deficiency is viewed as something their relationship can help with—fearful, disorganized, naïve, coarse, uncultured, etc. There is some sort of equilibrium between the partners' character traits that enable the individuals to initially be pleased with one another despite their perceived capacities and incapacities. Over time, events unbalance the equilibrium. Some frailties and incapacities only become apparent when life challenges the couple—jealousy, poor social judgment, unrealistic thinking. These newly realized traits for a time overshadow the positive features of the person. Recognition and acceptance of a partner's numerous character traits is one of the subtle tasks of adult development. It is often a private struggle that can eventually be resolved. Acceptance is often sensed by others as maturation or being realistic. The juxtaposition of a person's character traits creates irony—good and bad features coexist, one can be generous in some circumstances and not in others, one can talk about integrity and behave dishonestly, be loyal and flirt, be generally sweet but hard-nosed and mean about certain matters. Perhaps the most widely clinically appreciated irony is seen in relationships that form around the roles of the helpless and the rescuer. Over time, many people are turned off by the very traits of helplessness or superiority that were so pleasing earlier in their relationship.

A painfully shy, well-organized, obsessive, accomplished man married a warm, gregarious, disorganized woman in his field. Over time, his silent resentfulness over her continuing inability to take care of many things in her life became his reason for divorcing her.

Such mundane summaries of patients' lives are always oversimplifications. Character traits that alienate diminish the person's lovability, but they do not stand-alone. The partner's reaction is modulated by how this trait lines up with other positive and negative features. The fact that the alienating traits exist in the context of other features renders every relationship unique and every partner's sensibilities important to the willingness to bestow love.

While any clinician listening to patients describe what is annoying about their partners can generate a list of patterns that seem to thwart, frustrate, and diminish their aspiration to live and love harmoniously, these traits have not found their way into our psychological theories. Character traits that cause alienation are obvious to clinicians. Theories often invoke the remote and the unseen, helping the clinicians to formulate the problem from a different vantage point than the patient grasps. While theories may on occasion illuminate, they tend to bypass how embedded partners' character traits are in the context of other traits and social factors. As a result, I have found myself highly interested in what is causing my patients' relationships to deteriorate by seeking to help them to define the recurring behaviors that alienate them. These traits are not necessarily diagnostic items such as, extreme narcissism or paranoia, but they often are traits that clinicians recognize such as unfocused, impulsive, tangential, cruel, hyperbolic, optimistic, irresponsible, rationalizing, accusatory, etc.

The physical form of a partner may be aesthetically pleasing. Beauty is a major consideration for courtship processes, but it becomes less valuable over time. The couple's social presentation may appear to be ideal to others. Many aspects of their lives may function well, but within the privacy of their ongoing life, something is creating a significant negative appraisal. Character traits that alienate may consist of specific disapproved of behaviors as well as a growing awareness of the limits of the partner's capacities. It means something to the partner that even simple problems cannot be solved as a couple. It can be hurtful and worrisome when a partner is lied to about anything or watches a mate lie to others. It may be shocking that a partner does not share one's cherished religious ideas or political sensibilities or finds the mate to be vacuous. While every couple discovers that they have some differing interest in sports, recreation, entertainment and cultural activities, extreme differences in how pleasures are generated can dangerously increase the sense of separateness. Many couples struggle over what are boundaries for friendship patterns, flirtation, pornography use, and extra-dyadic sex.

Gradual realization of the divergent life goals of the partner, particularly when based on the recognition that the partner has a limited endowment of emotional expressiveness, intelligence, vocational effort, sexual capacity, or interest in relating to others explains a certain amount of grim acceptance of the partner. The relationship veers away from its former pleasures towards endurance. It would be lovely if relationships always provided a palpable degree of interest, pleasure and willingness to be sexual together along with caring and optimism about the future together. The reality for many partners, however, is that the character traits and incapacities of the partner propel love into a vegetative arrangement to attain other life goals, such as a two-parent family, financial security, and avoidance of aloneness.

Love is a self-management process. Within the privacy of one's mind, the partner's traits, capacities, and vulnerabilities are given meaning. These meanings are not static; they change over time with maturation. While the sequence remains correct throughout time—my partner behaves, I react, my partner reacts to my reaction, etc.—the reactions evolve because the same behavior comes to be seen in a different light. Meanings change. This category, character traits that alienate, reminds clinicians of the grand individuality of meaning making and its consequence: decision making. The same traits in two individuals may result in radically different decisions by their mates in bestowing love. We want to surrender to this individuality rather than to consider outcomes preordained by remote developmental factors.

Aggressive Behaviors

Aggressive behaviors can be considered as a character trait that alienates, but partner reactions are so intense that it is reasonable to consider these separately. Physical or verbal aggression challenges one's capacity to bestow love. Verbally abusive demeaning dominance patterns, sexual demandingness, or refusal to cooperate with a desired activity exhaust a partner's coping capacities and create a cynicism about love's ideals. When such patterns lead to the decision to divorce, the aggressive person often becomes more intensely passive-aggressive or directly uncooperative, taking pleasure in thwarting legal processes. Clinicians hear about these aggressive reactions from the divorcing partner, not the aggressive person.

There is another category of aggressive behaviors that clinicians generally do not see. These are the far more egregious. Clinicians learn of them from the media as they report sensational crimes or as perpetrators are dealt with by the judicial system. Criminal aggressiveness includes: sexual harassment; physical abuse; stalking of the partner or others; sexual abuse of minors within or outside the family; threat of or actual murder in response to a wife's intention to divorce;

or a partner's worsening jealous state. It may be useful to realize that before these tragedies occurred, far more subtle aggressive character traits were evident. These chilling traits constitute pathologies of love. They are so far beyond the ordinary conception of what love should be that both partners are often thought of as sick. Love is idealized as a positive, growth promoting interaction that mutually values each partner's individual needs and aspirations. Aggression towards one's mate, whether verbal, physical, or sexual, is a destructive force privately sensed as meanness, uncivilized, deteriorated, bad, or evil. The later is a term has been sanitized out of mental health discourse.

New Major Mental or Physical Illness

Of course, this is the vast category that health professionals of all ilks are immersed in. The onset of serious mental or physical illness can deteriorate affection, caring, sexual expression, and commitment in couples that previously had seemingly good-enough relationships. The ill person's loss of functional capacity and increasing self-centeredness and the burden of caring for the impaired person exhaust and exceed the partner's capacity. Through these forces, the illness converts a previous good-enough deal into a poor arrangement. The partner may be ashamed of his or her resentment. Even though fate changed the deal that they had, the general expectation of their commitment was to be there to provide care for this phase of life. Many a caregiver has to be educated about the ordinariness of the burdens of having a mentally or physically ill partner. The period of illness can be an ordeal, particularly when the relationship was previously compromised. On the other hand, some illness allows the partner to increase his or her affection for the afflicted one. The threat of loss creates a new appreciation of the past contributions to the partner's life and the limited time available to be present, kind, and helpful. While this sounds ideal, we are most interested in emphasizing how love is frequently eroded under conditions of serious lingering depression, multiple sclerosis, mania, stroke, Alzheimer's Disease, psychosis, etc.

Other Sources of the Loss of Love

Partners quickly discover that they have standards for bestowal of love only after these standards are violated. Private, within-the-family patterns such as the inability to remain cordial to extended family, emotional abandonment, or mistreatment of one's children or stepchildren and emotional inscrutability may ruin the original love that a partner had. The loss of love has many consequences.

Then there is the important matter that clinicians, even forensic specialists, avoid: criminality and what its various forms can do to change the trajectory of love. Like other sources of private relationship despair, criminal behaviors can generate hostility, anxiety, guilt, and internalized resentment. But unlike other items in Table 4.1, these often remain unmentioned to clinicians. If we consider criminality as a character trait, it would be considered as a large subcategory of character traits that alienate.

Current and past infidelity, through different mechanisms of destruction, is a notorious source of diminished ability to love a partner. Infidelity is such a common and powerful force in the evolution of an intimate relationship that it will be dealt with at greater length in Chapter Seven.

Love is a source of stabilization. It is an antidote for the strains of loneliness. It creates an auxiliary ego to be used as needed. This is commonly referred to as a support system. Gestures of support are not necessary most of the time. Support comes from the partner's presence and kindness during routine aspects of life. There are key moments, however, often involving pregnancy, delivery, illness, children's developmental accomplishments, and difficulties, death in family, etc. that are long remembered for a partner's absence or poor behaviors. These are long held onto within the partner's mind and tend to limit the sense of security and safety within the relationship.

These are love's interpersonal potentials: to accompany, assist, stabilize, and enrich the partner as life unfolds. Individuals may suddenly discover or gradually realize that what they previously assumed that they had in a partner was largely illusion. The shattering of assumptions about the partner seems to be sufficient to propel men and women into states of emotional illness. These states often get diagnosed and treated medically without the professional dwelling on the pathogenesis of the disorder. Even the inarticulate and those who only focus on their symptoms often intuitively grasp the relationship between their private love processes and their symptomatic state. Can they expect their mental health professional to be interested?

References

1 Lewis, C. S. (1960). *The four loves.* London: Jeoffrey Bles.
2 Singer, I. (2009). *Philosophy of love: A partial summing up.* Cambridge, Massachusetts: The MIT Press.
3 Sager, C. (1979). *Marriage contracts and couple therapy: Hidden forces in intimate relationships.* New York: Taylor & Francis.
4 Birch, J. (2012). *Confessions of a transsexual physician.* Boston: self-published by Jennifer Elizabeth Madden.
5 Levine, S., & Davis, L. (2002). What I did for love: Temporary returns to the male gender role. *International Journal of Transgenderism, 6*(4).

5

IMPEDIMENTS THAT LIMIT
A PERSON'S ABILITY
TO EXPRESS LOVE

We cannot but remain humble in our quest to understand how relationships fail. Given our need to oversimplify in order to merely discuss intimate interactions, and given the sheer number of forces that can undermine the pleasures of any union including the challenges from illness, accidents, children, and vocation, we should not expect to posit a theory to capture the phenomena at work. While we sometimes depend on theory or research to inform us, a heavy reliance on either may be misleading. Such reliance may only be our collective professional illusions that we grasp the subtle determinants of relationship outcome. In creating such illusions, we assume that life processes can be reduced to an individual developmental or behavioral essence. Perhaps this is generally true for gross factors, like early life abandonment, incest, or violence, but it is hard to fathom how it might be true for those that depend upon individual interpretation. If the readers judge this to be a reasonable chapter, I suspect they will be left with more awe than certainty of how the definable forces interact to generate our fates.

Functionally speaking, loving another is subjectively recognized by the ability to devote oneself to a chosen partner. The person recognizes an intense commitment to another. We never want to assume that individuals in new love relationships have similar degrees of, or capacities for, pleasure, interest, sexual desire, devotion, and optimism. In this chapter, we will try to understand the intrapsychic background for how these five dimensions of love decline within the index person. The index person can withdraw his or her love for four general reasons:

1. Because of negative appraisals from the partner
2. Because of negative appraisals of the partner
3. Because of internal forces having little to do with the partner
4. Because of external forces having little to do with the partner

The appraisal of the partner is an ongoing process that reflects the index person's current sensibilities. What the index person says about the partner may be true or not, but it typically reflects the speaker's unspoken thinking as well. For instance, "How do you expect me to have sexual desire for you after you have gained twenty pounds?" reveals much about the speaker. Maturation quietly evolves sensibilities

Table 5.1 Impediments That Limit the Index Person's Ability to Express Love

A. Awareness of Partner's Intense Dissatisfaction
B. Discovery of One's Alternative Gender Identity or Orientation
C. Acquired Sexual Dysfunctions
D. Sexual Excess Patterns
E. Paraphilias
F. Problematic Character Traits
G. Aggressive Behaviors
H. New Physical or Emotional Illness
I. Other Impediments
    a. Disrespect
    b. Prior Relationship Failure
    c. Partner Death
    d. Infidelity

about the partner, oneself, and the nature of love itself. Behavior is undertaken based on current sensibilities. As sensibilities change, the original action is seen in a new light. This new light is the fertile ground for regret.

Clarity about one's own contribution to relationship difficulties is difficult to achieve because of inherent defensiveness. It is easier to perceive one's partner's contributions, whether by behavior, behavioral lack, or character trait, than one's own. It is also easier to point to external forces such as, job loss, in-law meddling, and prejudice. We should recall, however, that after one or more relationship failures that are initially blamed on partners and circumstances, people are known to conclude that they do not have the capacities to live harmoniously with another person. They then can acknowledge that, in their case, the concept of pathology of love applies because they have proven to themselves that they possess it. We are seeking to define such pathologies so as to be more useful to the index person.

Table 5.1, an outline of Part 3 of the Compendium of Love's Pathologies, focuses on major reasons that a person withdraws his or her love from a partner. Most of its categories are familiar because they were discussed in Chapter Four from the partner's perspective. We are now entering an even more complex aspect of the compendium in seeking to grasp what internal considerations limit a person from sustaining love for a partner. These considerations are intensely private.

Awareness of Partner's Intense Dissatisfaction

People vary in the ease with which they will share the minor resentments, disappointments, and frustrations of daily life with a partner. If a partner is expressive of these transient negative experiences, the index person may dismissively view it as the partner's character trait, be repeatedly annoyed at the stream of reminders of personal shortcomings or respond by internally cancelling obligations to the partner. If a partner is rarely expressive of temporary matters, the person may have the illusion that he or she is quite pleasing and beloved. The range of attitudes about the partner's ordinary frustrations is a reminder that all people interpret how their partners regard them. Artistry of partnership may be characterized by consistent positive regard and tactful expressions of frustration. Each member of the couple needs to comprehend that frustrations are inevitable in relationships.

A new relationship psychology emerges after a person realizes that the partner is deeply unhappy, particularly after the partner acknowledges contemplating ending the union. This is typically stated during an argument and often is accompanied by *I did not mean it* after the argument is over. But it was said, and often it adds to the numerous times divorce was threatened during such disturbing moments. While clinicians see couples that begin conjoint therapy under these circumstances, most individuals do not. Rather, they find themselves becoming cold, withdrawn, disinterested, and less cooperative. The hardening of the heart toward the partner is based on the anticipation of ultimate abandonment. While it comes downstream from the factors that originally alienated the partner, it further devitalizes the relationship, lowers the expectations for the future, and often is a prelude to divorce. This is why this cold reaction should be thought of as an ominous response—one of the final steps in the more subtle pathologies of love.

Many patients have told me in front of their spouses that they are primarily angry with the partner because the partner is unhappy with them. Their partners offer numerous complaints over time about the index person's behaviors (character traits). The index person sadly utters, "I did not think them that serious." Even though the couple is in the therapist's office, the partner's anger at being ignored for so long may make the index person feel hopeless. Here is where therapist's skill comes in. We can demonstrate an interest in each other's subjectivities in such a way as to not think that the end has arrived. We model a noncritical comprehension of each person's perspective. Our manner conveys an understanding that appreciation of one another's internal world is the missing bridge to their lost emotional connection. Apology can be appreciated in a different way. Psychological intimacy is the pathway to love.[1] Creating it in the session and teaching how to attain it are what couple's therapists sell for a living.

However, without regaining psychological intimacy, the index person's new prideful, rejecting formality one day erupts in an irrational explosion of rage. Between the initial awareness of partner bitterness and the explosion, the index person's grim state affectively calls up all previous rejections and reverberates with the partner's lack of enjoyment of the person.

Discovering One's Orientation or Gender Identity

This category delineates two of the numerous facets of our lives that evolve over time—gender identity and orientation. The subjective changes within heterosexuals do not command much clinical attention. This is not so for the other

4–8% of the population. Sexual minorities come out to themselves and others as part of the process of consolidating their gender identity or orientation. These processes are frequently not finished by the beginning of adulthood. Coming out begins as an internal self label and may or may not extend to friends and lovers, the larger world, and one's complete family of origin.

We are concerned with pairings in which the index person develops a new sexual identity. The person often claims continuing love for the partner. This love is typically characterized by limited sexual behavior together and the loss of sexual desire for the partner. There is often a burning sexual desire for an experience with another class of persons. The right to express the new genuine self feels profoundly entitled; it promises a new level of happiness without plaguing hesitation, anxiety, and sadness. The person articulates regret for the disruption brought to the partner, their children, parents, and siblings. More intense regret awaits a change in sensibilities, familial adversity, or the first personal failure in the new life style. Despite the regret, many remain happy that the transition was accomplished. Regret is not a present or absent phenomenon nor is it a permanent emotion.

To unsuspecting family members, the transitioning person may appear to be behaving impulsively. There is, of course, always a long backstory. With all the media attention to coming out and the general recommendation that a person should transition, it is important to realize that some people choose to contain their gender or orientation struggles and bear the angst that comes with this adaptation. It is quite an ethical problem: Do I pursue my happiness in the life I have imagined, or do I privately bear my frustration to avoid injuring my immediate and extended family?[2] Regret accompanies either resolution.

A 50-year-old married father of three, a successful engineer, has used obligation, devotion to work, and immersion in church activities to cope with his private struggles to suppress a wish to live as a woman. He has never informed his wife about it so as to not upset her. He has been doctoring for anxiety periodically for four years but only recently revealed its source to his therapist who referred him to me.

Doctor: What would you like to do about your gender?
Patient: I'd like to live as a woman, I really would, but I know I won't. I just can't. I just want to talk about it with someone who is knowledgeable and comfortable. You have no idea how hard it is to find a doctor who knows anything about this.
Doctor: Well, I'm glad to discuss this with you. Where should we begin?
Patient: I really love my wife and kids and would not do anything to harm them.
Doctor: Even if it means sacrificing your consistent desire to socially express yourself as a woman?

Patient: Well . . . it is not that consistent. It began in earnest about five years ago when my daughter graduated from college and got established in a new city. Before that, although it was always there somewhere, sometimes it got worse than others. I was miserable as a teenager. Anyway, I'm not mad at my wife. She is a good person. She did not cause this, and she does not deserve any disruption in her life, particularly just two years after her cancer operation.

Doctor: You sound like a very responsible person.

Patient: I try to be, but sometimes I think I will lose my mind. When I am not busy, I feel so depressed and withdrawn from my wife because I can't be me.

Doctor: Do you have sex together?

Patient: Yes, but I don't think I enjoy it too much because I feel I am not there. I think sometimes I am her during sex. My wife says she enjoys sex. She often says she loves me but I feel I give her so little.

Doctor: Am I right when I say that I bet your wife, children, and your church might say that you give a great deal to others?

Patient: Yes, but that is not really true. I help out in the community doing what I like to do. I think I do it so regularly because thinking about others distracts me from wishing I was a woman.

Doctor: Well, women often are quite helpful to others.

Patient: (Smiling), Thank you. . . . I feel like I am so strange, my desire is so strange.

Doctor: Well, when I began as a psychiatrist, such desires were strange to me as well. Now I see that many people struggle over how to integrate their masculine and feminine elements into a cohesive sexual identity. So you may understand when I say, you don't seem strange to me.

The most common sexual identity transitions involve longing for homosexual experience, but transitions also include a desire for heterosexual marriage among gay and lesbian identified individuals.[3] The latter circumstances do not get publicity. No one knows how common any of these struggles are in the population. When clinicians get to see them, however, the persons who want to transition often portray themselves as "going through the motions," "acting," or "withdrawn and lost in my fantasies." Individuals like the engineer often initially present themselves as consistently struggling with their sexual identify. As we get to know them better, the struggles are described as waxing and waning, sometimes for long periods of time. When they heat up, pleasure and interest in the partner often is replaced by depressive self-absorption. They feel too deprived to have much to give to the partner. They are preoccupied with creating a genuine self. Subjectively, they care less about their family. Their family, like the engineer's wife and children, may not notice! When we initially see them, optimism about their future is based on living the aspired to gender or orientation. If they choose to undergo a social change, they usually leave their partners and children. When families muster support, it often is far more ambivalent and inconsistent than the index person realizes.

Acquired Sexual Dysfunctions

Acquired sexual dysfunctions are related to love in two ways: They either are the result of loss of love for the partner or, having a different pathogenesis, they create new obstacles to feeling and expressing love. It is remarkable that love has rarely been invoked to explain sexual dysfunction in forty-plus years of professional discourse on the subject. New dysfunctions can be precipitated and maintained by organic factors. Mental health professionals need to be particularly mindful of the capacity of many of our medications, particularly those with serotonergic properties, to induce sexual dysfunction. This large category of organic influences poses new obstacles to feeling and expressing love by creating the sense of personal inadequacy and sexual avoidance. Particularly in the last half of adult life, factors such as atherosclerosis of the pudental artery or cancer chemotherapy afflict individuals with a variety of impairments that diminish the physiological capacity for sexual pleasure. Partner sex may eventually cease after sexual intensity, frequency, and satisfaction decline. As this system of nurturance dissipates, often the second system, psychological intimacy, does as well. The couple moves into a companionate phase. While some couples accomplish this gracefully with sadness, humor, and perspective, many others get into relationship trouble because they lack the capacity to discuss this important change. The silent unilateral withdrawal from sex leaves the partner deprived and resentful and may leave the inarticulate index person embarrassed and defensive. Their affects then may play out in some other interpersonal arena. Many asexual couples with organic dysfunctions can be helped to regain some aspects of their sexual life together. There is much written about the sexual rehabilitation of cancer patients, but the interested mental health professional's acknowledgement of the importance of the topic is itself fundamentally at least as important as any suggestions for coping with these organic dysfunctions. Physicians may have little to offer many cancer patients other than moisturizers and lubricants for women and an erectogenic agent for men. People have to overcome their assumptions that the erect penis and the moist vagina are the only legitimate sexual organs.

New Premature Ejaculation

These men who used to have markedly better control of their arousal in the vagina seem baffled as to the source of lost capacity to provide an adequate intercourse experience. Single men who are starting anew with a partner would seem to only require a bit more time to regain control over their arousal. Those that seek our assistance have not improved with time, however. Many are worried about being a pleasing partner because of their previous partner's dissatisfaction. Ironically, this anxiety puts them in a different erotic zone from the partner who is focusing on the pleasures of a new emotional connection while he is preoccupied with when he will ejaculate. Usually, experienced partners are quite supportive, nonchalant, or optimistic about the intercourse per se.

Therapy helps these men understand the source of their anxiety and tries to get them to participate in the sensuality of early bonding regardless of their time in the vagina. A medication may help, but if the man cannot attend to the therapist's advice, the problem may continue as the partner loses interest and the pattern just repeats itself until he gives up on intimate relationships.

Partnered men may develop this pattern after cardiac illness because they are afraid of precipitating another episode of arrhythmia or angina.[4] Other partnered men develop this pattern because of private derision for their partner.

A financially stable man developed premature ejaculation after his wife of 23 years, always insecure about her appearance, was arrested for shoplifting. She then confessed to him about her longstanding pattern. Trapped by his wish not to add to her mortification, but smoldering with resentment, the symptom appeared. She insists that her arrest has cured her. "Until this happened I thought her preoccupation with fashion was just a woman-thing. "Clearly, she has some sort of problem. Do you know how much the lawyer cost?" At our visit six months following her arrest, he presented preoccupied with his sexual incapacity and did not fully perceive the relationship between the two events.

The persistence of new premature ejaculation usually induces the man to slink away from the sexual experience. Preoccupied with his performance failure, sex is no longer fun. Therapists ought to be able to help with this pattern before it transforms the relationship into an asexual one.

Erectile Dysfunction

Psychogenic impotence, as this dysfunction has been known for millennia, is associated with considerable anxiety. Its source usually comes into focus as the history is taken, and that enables the therapist to base the treatment on its personal or interpersonal sources. A typical consequence is the silent avoidance of sex or, in the case of unattached men, their mysterious withdrawal from courtship. In established heterosexual or homosexual relationships, the man may remain consistently kind and considerate but sex tends to disappear without much discussion other than the promise to get help if it does not get better soon by itself. The partner may actually believe that he is working too hard, has too much stress in his life, or is just too fatigued, but he knows that there is something else behind his difficulty. He may delay dealing directly with the psychological source by seeking consultation with a general physician or urologist, who will, of course, provide a PDE-5i medication. The patient ignores the fact that he can get a lasting erection under circumstances other than with his partner for intercourse. Considering the rapidity with which a knowledgeable clinician and partner can perceive its origins, we must conclude that he is too frightened to confront the underlying issue, which often involves the processes of love.

A 45-year-old handsome man who has long frustrated his attractive wife by his quiet emotionally inexpressive self lost potency after his wife informed him that she was thinking about having an affair and ending their marriage. He chose to believe her that nothing had yet happened, but for the next two years before they sought therapy he could not maintain an erection with her, even after her threat of divorce was quickly rescinded. He could only report that he was anxious about performance. It took him six sessions of therapy before he was able to acknowledge affectively that her near affair and her complaints about his unemotional nature had undermined his self-confidence. His kind, blunt, frustrated wife understood what happened to him even though he did not. When successful intercourse returned to their lives, he continued to have difficulty expressing his feelings other than being anxious. "But I am getting better at it!" His wife agreed and emphasized that she will be able to love him more if he shares himself more.

A 60-year-old man whose first wife died of cancer when he was 52 did not date for six years in part because he did not feel like it and in part because he feared his young son would be upset by it. Never impotent with his wife, he did not want to have sex prior to marriage with his fiancée. When he married, he could not maintain an erection and soon avoided all sexual contact after he failed to improve with two PDE-5i drugs. He insisted that the problem was neither a sense of loyalty to his wife or nor associated with religious issues. Able to erect with infrequent masturbation, he only could express frustration with his problem. He was completely baffled by its presence because he so much loved and enjoyed his new wife. He would agree to only monthly therapy sessions and dropped out after the fourth one, dissatisfied with the lack of erections during suggested sensual interactions. His wife was happy to be with him but was sad about their brother-sister relationship. She reported that she had talked to herself about engaging in sex because she did not feel wanted by him, despite his words to the contrary. "I know he loves me, but I still feel resentful about our courtship." I would have gladly had intercourse before marriage with Bill."

While it seems clear that psychogenic erectile dysfunction is an impediment to love, the more basic pathology is the inability to know and share what the man thinks and feels. While we glibly refer to such men as unaware, I frequently find myself suspecting that the feelings are known but too embarrassing to share. When the man is encouraged to offer a hypothesis as to the source of the problem, after a few I-don't-knows, he often provides a cogent rough suggestion that we can quickly refine. I must admit that I suspect that men whose behaviors do not match their histories, such as Bill, are lying to me about their sexual histories.

Acquired Hypoactive Sexual Desire Disorder

Well into marriage or a gay relationship, erectile dysfunction and low sexual desire often seem to run together. Erectile dysfunction (ED) may come first or second in sequence of symptoms. As there are medications for ED, therapists and physicians are now apt to offer them as a first approach to the problem, particularly since there are no medications available for men with low desire who have normal testosterone and prolactin. This sometimes results in collusion between the doctor seeking a rapid improvement and the patient seeking to avoid an uncomfortable truth such as, *I may love her (him) but I certainly don't like how she (he) behaves with me and with others. To tell you the truth, I don't know what love is, anyway.* The reasons for no longer liking the partner might be anything, but these patterns are experienced as character traits: she stirs up trouble with others, he is annoying, she has to be the center of attention, he is obnoxious with wait staff or anyone who works for us, she treats my family rudely, he is emotionally inconstant, she is too demanding of our children, he is not honest, etc.

Modern medical treatment of ED treats the symptom as it is a stand-alone problem. But therapists recognize that psychogenic ED may be a downstream manifestation of earlier relationship dissatisfaction. Men with low desire and ED, fearful of disrupting their lives by expressing much dissatisfaction with the partner, seem to develop these symptoms because they deny the meaning to them of their partners' aggravating character traits or their own past secret behaviors. Therapists should not pretend that low sexual desire can be treated effectively without understanding its psychological pathogenesis. Realistically, patients should not expect physicians, other than the occasional psychiatrist, to be skillful in dealing with love problems that present as ED/Hypoactive Sexual Desire Disorders. Many cases of Hypoactive Sexual Desire Disorder are cured by partner change.[5]

Inability to Ejaculate with a Partner

We occasionally see a man who remains excited enough by sexual intercourse to maintain an erection but who is untrusting of his safety in ejaculating within or outside of the partner. We know this is psychogenic because he readily ejaculates with masturbation. Men who have lost their ability to ejaculate inside the partner seem to have become more sensitive about the danger of physical closeness or have become frightened of emotional intensity in general. Their new paranoid or obsessive-compulsive pathology of love is also a downstream manifestation of an earlier drama in their lives. Men who develop this pattern almost always had excellent intravaginal control beginning with their first intercourse. It is not uncommon to eventually learn that the symptom followed a partner's affair.[6] Most mental health professionals know to look carefully at the list of medications a man with this new symptom is currently taking. Many agents can make orgasm more difficult to attain.

Women's Sexual Interest/Arousal Disorder

This vast topic, the subject of numerous recent frustrated searches for a medication cure, creates many questions but few answers. Generalizations about women's sexual dysfunctions, to be trustworthy, must stress a broad range of sexual interests, capacities, and experiences. Women's sexual capacities are often potentials that are not met because of developmental and cultural disadvantages. Women often discover their peak sexual physiological capacities later than men. They have a deep intuitive grasp, compared to men, of the contextual nature of their willingness to be sexual. These contexts may be biological, psychological, interpersonal, or cultural.[7]

Most of the women who complain of low sexual desire and/or sexual arousal difficulties reference their former lives before children, work, or parental burdens. Many are distressed because their partners are distressed, and they fear the consequences of continuing in their muted sexual state. Some of these women are not ready to state that they no longer love their partners. They may, however, say *I love him but am no longer in love with him. I don't know what love is. Or, I guess I love her but. . . .* Over time, of course, they have gotten to know their partner's capacities and incapacities in ways that they did not previously grasp when sex was fine. This may be the ultimate reason that their sexual ardor has dampened.

Professionals close to the pharmaceutical industry assume that there is an undiscovered physiological explanation for the problem. The administration of testosterone is the current candidate for reversing diminished interest, arousal, and responsiveness. All medication trials involving women's sexual desire/arousal are characterized by high placebo response rates, which adds to the burden of proof in randomized clinical trials.[8] Diverse therapists have expressed optimism about helping women with education, reassurance, and theory-based interventions.[9] Individual psychotherapy often reveals women's private dissatisfactions, conflicts with partner, or issues manifested since adolescence. Since there is no objective way to ascertain the etiology of this dysfunction, the clinician must work out the pathogenesis case by case. Many therapists, after working in depth with women with this problem, wonder whether their patients' fluctuating or low sexual drive states and disinterest in interacting sexually are simply normal or an epiphenomenon of subtle states of depression. Many women themselves eventually conclude that they don't love their partners or that they have lost the commitment to or obligation to have sex because of what has transpired between them. It is a cultural bias to more readily look for the lack of love for a partner among women than among men with the same disorder. I prefer to deemphasize gender and seek explanations for desire and arousal problems in the meanings that the index person has given to their observations about their partners.

It often takes a little time to share these private meanings with the therapist. The therapist has to demonstrate interest by the type of questions asked. Medical health professionals focus on dysfunction and its "treatment." The therapist, in contrast, in interested in the woman's motives to have sex and motives to avoid having sex.[10] We focus on her subjective experience of sexual drive, the difference between her masturbatory life and her partnered life, and the degree of nonsexual pleasure she has with her partner. It sounds to the average woman like we are discussing the dimensions of her experiences of loving.

Loss of Orgasmic Capacity

As women experience their sexual physiological downturn with menopause, orgasm may be increasingly difficult to attain. The body seems to betray the woman after years of regular reliable orgasmic attainment. Interpersonally, orgasm is often a highly valued outcome for the partner. The question for clinicians is whether women with this dysfunction have developed a motive to withhold the gift of orgasm as a punishment or as a reflection of the lack of trust. Clinicians need to be on the alert for medication-induced loss of orgasmic capacity since this is quite common among those on SSRIs, SNRIs, and opioid medications.[11]

Sexual Excess Patterns

There is no subtlety about these psychopathologies of love. They involve heterosexual, homosexual and paraphilic individuals, and while they are not exclusively male problems, they are predominantly so.[12] Among coupled heterosexuals, they are characterized by preoccupation with women other than the current partners. Among the unattached, the patterns seem to preclude finding a noncommercial partner. The women who are of interest are generally young, voluptuous, and artful in portraying pleasure in arousing men. The men create a pretend world in which there is an illusion of a relationship. The patterns range from behaviors thought to be normal in unattached young men to those that are conspicuous distractions from mental deterioration. It is hard to imagine that most partners, female or male, would remain calm about these secret patterns if they knew the details. When they are discovered, the partner's first reaction is a variation of "You are sick!" The term sexual addiction likens the behavior to self-destructive substance abuse patterns. The shock of discovery ends some relationships, lowers expectations in others, and for yet others generates compassion for the illness behind the behaviors. The latter creates a reprieve from unforgiveable censure by granting the sick role. Compassion and professional treatment only delay coming to grips with the meaning of the pattern and the nature of the thought processes among those who have immersed themselves in these promised pleasures.

It is what is underneath these patterns that is of interest at the moment. It is far easier to deal with the shock of discovery for the man and his partner than to acknowledge that this pattern was a solution to a more basic difficulty in loving. In listening to the man describe the activities that he feels he is unable to stop, I ask myself: Is an actual person involved? Is there face-to-face contact? What sexual behavior is being purchased? Does the man become emotionally attached to the woman? The answers are clarifying. We want to eventually be able to understand why he does this, so I ask the questions. This sets the stage for the development of a hypothesis that he can understand.

The short-term goal of sexual excess patterns or "sexual addiction," unlike an affair where a man and a partner have become attached to one another, is arousal, not attachment. Some men defend and celebrate these behaviors as evidence of normal heterosexual or homosexual masculinity. To me they seem adolescent. There is an early adolescent phase when sex is longed for because the female or male form is distractingly alluring. Sexual behavior symbolizes for the teenager emancipation from parents and childhood, but he is not yet mature enough to enter into a multifaceted relationship with a real person. The goal of these patterns is masturbatory orgasm or orgasm without attachment to the partner.

A dysthymic compulsive middle-aged professional went to a strip club with a friend for the first time and fell in love with the place. Four months later he was discovered to be attending 3–4 times per week, befriending the strippers with large tips and gifts and feeling he was "big man on campus." His wife characterized him as chronically disinterested in sex and emotional closeness. He has built his life around work, very little else has mattered to him over the years.

A married man with a clear-cut sexual addiction is usually aware that he does not want to participate in sex with his wife; it is the source of anxiety, dysfunction, and disappointment. The specific reasons vary with the circumstances. Many of these men say that they love their wives. But their love is a speech, an attempt to reassure and placate, a concept based more on years and activities than a series of acts of caring, closeness, and compassion. As they come to realize their emotional abandonment of their mate, their concept of love may deepen.

You screw female and male prostitutes for years and yet you say you love me. Forgive me if I fail to understand what you mean by love!"

Paraphilias

Let us just assume for our purposes that most paraphilic men have their paraphilia as a consequence of early or late childhood trauma, typically involving a poor quality relationship with a parent, an abuse process or experience, or a specific traumatizing humiliation. As a consequence, the adult is primarily interested in arousal with a partner under specific conditions that relate to his earlier repressed or camouflaged traumatic background. Paraphilia is a sexual disorder that varies in the degree to which it precludes more conventional behaviors. Those with less compelling forms can attach to and love a partner. The trouble is the partner's ultimate dissatisfaction with complying with his unique sexual needs, limiting the desire to participate in sex with him. This induces his resentment and sense of deprivation. These forces compete with the paraphilic's loving processes. When paraphilic behaviors take on intensity or compulsivity, they can lead to infidelity, sexual excess patterns, or coercing mates to participate sexually with strangers. Paraphilia challenges the man's capacity to love to the extent that his needs for his unique sexual gratification fill his mind with anger, guilt, and sadness and create unexplained withdrawal from the emotional connection to the partner.

Problematic Character Traits

DSM-IV instructed clinicians to think of three groups of personality *disorders*: those that involved oddness or eccentricity—paranoid, schizoid, schizotypal (Cluster A); those that involved drama or emotionality—borderline, narcissistic, histrionic, antisocial (Cluster B); and those that involved anxiety or fear—avoidant, obsessive-compulsive, dependent (Cluster C).[13] Psychometric testing tends to describe personality *traits* in these same terms when they do not rise to the intense level of a disorder. We don't usually think about what these designations mean for the processes of love for the person who bears the diagnosis. It is much easier to imagine the impact of these traits on the partner than to understand how the index individuals regard their partners. When psychoanalytic authors emphasize the juxtaposition of love and aggression, transference of resentments from parents to spouses, and marital reenactment of attachment problems with a parent, we are impressed that how a person is loved as a child may have a great deal to do with how he and she will love as an adult. We don't think there is anything like a 1:1 correlation. Yet, the body of clinical experience over a century creates a strong impression that healthy loving as an adult is fostered by a happy, secure, respectful love within the family of origin. Personality disorders and traits have significance for relationship evolution and the index person's ability to love. The reader can pick any one of these disorders and try to imagine what this person may need in order to feel love for the partner.

There are far more problematic character traits than are listed in any version of the DSM. Problematic character traits are perceived by others, not the index person. Partners may complain: *I can't stand that she talks endlessly, that he only talks about himself, that she is constantly complaining, that he is so mean to our children, that she is so scatter-brained, that he is indecisive, that she is always sure about everything, that he promises more than he delivers, that she is not socially engaging*, etc. The index person is just being him or herself, doing what comes naturally. How does having these traits influence the index person's felt love for the partner? How does having such problematic traits influence the partner's perception of the kind, caring, supportive behaviors that the index person also demonstrates? It is very difficult to discern the answers.

The couple had an arrangement that worked well enough to get them to a commitment stage. The index person most likely had the problematic character trait during the formative processes of their relationship. That trait was balanced by far more positive factors or enjoyed for its own sake. *I like it that she talks so easily; it complements my quiet nature. I find his comments about himself refreshing because in my family such talk seemed to be a sin. Her complaints help me to appreciate that there is a hierarchy of quality in all things and she has enabled me to aspire to the higher end of things,* etc. Such interacting attitudes enable the love to develop. Over time, these persistent traits may erode the pleasure in the union. The index person notices that criticism of what used to be acceptable is now forthcoming. The danger here is that the awareness of partner's dissatisfaction may cause the index person's heart to harden.

Life typically becomes more complex and demanding over time. Work, children, money, and family obligations vie for the limited time and energy of couples. Their mutual nurturance tends to take a back seat to these more acute demands. It is the wise and enviable couple that can recognize and maintain their value to one another in the face of new demands. They must grapple with a central issue: Can we remain appreciative, supportive, kind, respectful, cooperative, sexually receptive, interested, and articulate with one another?

If we just pay attention to what our patients say about their partners, therapists get the impression that it is typically the partner with some problematic trait who is the problem. The therapist may be able to encourage the person to wonder what it is like to be his or her partner. This introduces the idea that the same central issue applies to the index person as well as the partner. After all, the index person has capacities and incapacities, warmth and resentment, interest and disinterest, praise and complaints, prudence and injudiciousness. Love is transacted daily through a series of mundane interactions, which either may underscore the pleasures of being a couple or reinforce the notion that the deal has become a bad one. The therapist may find a kind way of raising the question of whether the patient has remained appreciative, supportive, kind, respectful, cooperative, sexually receptive, interested, and articulate.

The trouble for therapists is that we cannot gain access to the private process of love in the index person. We hear bits and pieces of it, particularly when the deal seems to be souring. The process, which some prefer to think of as unconscious, is continuous, and much of it is quite conscious. Relationships consist of a series of moments. Unhappy spouses speak of particularly unhappy moments when their partner mishandled certain meaningful situations. Regretful spouses speak of moments when they mishandled the situation whose meaning they have only come to understand. Apologizing often helps when the mishandled moment has been quickly recognized.

Aggressive Behaviors

By temperament—that is, inherent tendencies in the self, some individuals are quite aggressive within their families and within their intimate relationships. This takes many forms, such as interpersonal forcefulness, punishment of those who do not cooperate, coercion, poor frustration tolerance, selfishness, threats of violence, episodic violence, etc. Families have a chance to work on these traits during the index person's childhood, but many such traits persist despite the efforts of parents and educators. When they create some tragedy and hurt or maim another, we may think they are mentally ill or need to be segregated from society as criminals. Hopefully, most domestic aggressiveness does not result in the tragedies that interest the media.

From the index person's vantage point, the violence is provoked by frustration. The partner does not understand what needs to be done. Of course, this strikes others as narcissistic and lacking in insight. The index person's aggression may be provoked by substance abuse, most notoriously alcohol, vocational inadequacies, gambling losses, or any predicament outside the home. The spouse and children are scapegoats for the person's frustrations. These aggressive domestic behaviors are so obviously antithetical to basic notions of protecting one's spouse and children from harm that it is hard to imagine that the aggressive person ever feels warmly disposed to others. Psychiatrists medicate intermittent explosiveness; courts send mildly violent people for anger management therapy, and therapists see couples after violent episodes. These men often aspire to love but do not seem to know how. One of the reasons to emphasize love more in our work is to recognize when a person needs to learn how to love and when a person can be inspired to behave better. Love, like justice, can be an inspirational concept that provides a goal to work towards as part of a rehabilitation effort. This may generate a different approach to some aggressive character types. Love can be the source of hope for individuals and their partners. We must, however, guard against naïve optimism.

New Physical or Emotional Illness

We should look at love as a state that may blossom best for most people in states of health, both physical and mental. Health allows the couple to focus on each other in a mutually nurturing way. Our fate, sadly, is not to remain healthy forever. Many people have serious chronic impediments to their capacities to be in the world. We take our turns being ill, dysfunctional, relatively dependent and helpless, and disappointed that we are now less than what we were. Some can love under these conditions because their losses help them to appreciate their lives, maximize what capacities that remain, and to feel gratitude for the care they receive from their partners. But illness also makes individuals irritable, impolite, demanding, self-absorbed, and anxious. They may have little pleasantness or gratitude to provide to their partners who notice, of course, that their mate is not the same. If the illness is chronic and the index person is not able to contain his or her internal misery, a changed relationship ensues. Illness, per se, does not ensure the loss of loving behaviors. Warmth, kindness, gratitude, and interest in the spouse go a long way to ease the burdens of the caregiving spouse and allow the afflicted person to continue to feel the sensations of love.

Other Impediments

It is far easier to love a partner when the person is respect-worthy. Whereas a couple that is immersed in a sociopathic lifestyle may have great respect for the criminal capacities of a partner, the discovery that one's spouse has been active in shady dealings may cause ordinary peoples' hearts to harden. Many behaviors, character traits really, over time come to be appreciated as not up to one's personal standards.

Love him, hell no! Divorce him, I wish. I stay with him for the lifestyle. I don't want to be alone; we have an active social life. But he is a slovenly, dishonest, spineless cheater. I don't want to have any sexual contact with him anymore. Let him run with his girlfriends. I don't care! I used to love him. Now I can't remember why, except that the sex was great, and I only saw that he was under his parent's control. Gradually, he made me a nervous wreck through his unkept promises. It took me too long to realize what a snake he always has been.

So many topics can be discussed under Other Impediments. Individuals can grow protective of themselves from disappointments in love so that they do not want to try again. After two divorces, an individual may think that he or she has poor judgment, that marriage is an impossible arrangement, or that he or she never wants the misery that stems from disappointing a partner. Loneliness is the lesser of two evils as far as they are now concerned. Similarly, there are recurring reasons why a person may not be willing to love again following a spouse's death. These are not mutually exclusive reasons.

1. I have had such a good marriage, why would I settle for something less?
2. I am not finished with the grief process and being involved with another person is actually offensive to me. I am not ready to think about it.
3. I had to endure so much with my spouse, in health and in illness, that the idea of being committed and obligated again is not appealing.
4. Men (or women) want more than I want to give. I want my freedom to be me.
5. I'm a realistic. The chances of getting married again are slim. Who would want me now? I am prepared to live out my life as best as I can.

Nonetheless, the aspiration to love and to be loved is strong throughout life. While we don't know the time course of the resistance to exposing oneself to the dangers of courtship for any individual, we do know two factors that often change these attitudes. The first one, time, is impressive in how it silently changes one's sensibilities. Earlier in life we called this maturation, but perhaps we ought to remind ourselves that it is a mystery how we evolve. It is less important in the final analysis to know how time works than to know that it affects our understanding, feelings, attitudes, and willingness to intimately know others.

The second factor, a specific person, can be more powerful than time. A divorced or widowed person, dead set against any internal aspiration to be with another person for a host of well defined reasons, meets someone who is not only interested but has a trait or two that is deeply compatible and compelling. The tectonic plates of one's mind shift. One becomes receptive again, willing to bear the risks for the promises of love.

I was a mess. My husband died of pancreatic cancer four months before I met him. I was deeply depressed and uncertain about everything. My adult children had a bitter fight and would not talk to one another. One son thought I took the other's side and would not talk to me or let me see my grandchildren. I had to manage our business alone during a down cycle. During my husband's last months, as if his dying wasn't enough, I could hardly attend to my dear mother who was shell shocked with grief over what was happening to her family. After the funeral, my husband's last year was running through my brain nonstop. The last thing I wanted was another man.

Along came this person who saw me from afar and asked a friend to introduce him. I declined. Four months! I'm not ready. It was obscene. He persisted. My friends checked him out and gave me a positive report. We met for coffee. He was very nice. He listened kindly to everything I told him. He was entertaining. He had lost his mother with whom he was close a year before. Imagine that: a man who loves and cares diligently for his mother during her terminal cancer! He wanted to meet my mother after our second time together. They got along instantly. She perked up and encouraged me about him. He seemed to adore both of us. He never resisted spending time with her. He wanted to be with me all the time. He wore my resistance down because I had such a good time with him. I felt alive again. We liked the same things . . . with a few exceptions. He agreed to try them. He let me talk about my husband; he told me about his ex. We shared stories of our difficult children. He thought me beautiful. I gave in. We married on the one-year anniversary of our meeting. I'm still happy, but I need help with getting my son back.

It is humbling to recall that this woman's experience was understood hundreds of years before she was born. Shakespeare grasped the power of another person's romantic interest to convert disinterest in love into erotic fire. He created characters that were vehemently against love only to be transformed by the ardor of another's attraction. He helped us to see the humor in it and to doubt the permanence of well-articulated negative positions on love. We laugh when the transformations occur even as the characters are duped into thinking the other was smitten. Beatrice and Benedict from *Much Ado About Nothing* are now immortal representatives of the power of perceiving that one is the object of another's love.[14] If only mental health professionals could convey these fundamental aspects of receptivity to love with half the grace and clarity.

References

1 Levine, S. (2006). *Demystifying love: Plain talk for the mental health professional.* (Chapter 4). New York: Routledge.

2 Klosterman, C. (2013, 3 February). Transition point. *New York Times Magazine*, 13.

3 Diamond, L. (2008). *Sexual fluidity: Understanding women's sexual love and desire.* Cambridge: Harvard University Press.

4 Althof, S. (2005). Psychological treatment strategies for rapid ejaculation: Rationale, practical aspects, and outcome. *World Journal of Urology, 23*, 89–92.

5 Levine, S. (2009). Male hypoactive sexual desire disorder. In R. Balon & R.T. Segraves (Eds.), *Clinical manual of sexual disorders* (pp. 161–184). Washington, DC: American Psychiatric Press.

6 Waldinger, M. (2010). Premature and delayed ejaculation. In S. B. Levine, C. B. Risen & S.E. Althof (Eds.), *Handbook of clinical sexuality for mental health professionals* (pp. 267–292). New York: Routledge.

7 Basson, R., & Brotto, L. (2009). Disorders of sexual desire and subjective arousal in women. In R. Balon & R.T. Segraves (Eds.), *Clinical manual of sexual disorders* (pp. 119–160). Washington, DC: American Psychiatric Press.

8 Bradford A., & Meston, C.M. (2009). Placebo response in the treatment of women's sexual dysfunctions: A review and commentary. *Journal of Sex and Marital Therapy, 35*, 164–181.

9 Leiblum, S. (2010). *Sexual desire disorders: A casebook.* New York: Guilford Press.

10 Meston, C.M., Hamilton, L.D., & Harte, C.B. (2009). Sexual motivation in women as a function of age. *Journal of Sexual Medicine, 6*, 3305–3319.

11 Meston, C.M. (2004). Disorders of orgasm in women. *Journal of Sexual Medicine, 1*, 66–68.

12 Turner, M. (2008). Female sexual compulsivity: A new syndrome. *Psychiatric Clinics of North America, 31*, 713–727.

13 American Psychiatric Association. (1994). *Diagnostic and statistical manual-IV-TR*, Washington, DC: American Psychiatric Press.

14 Shakespeare, W. (1997). Much ado about nothing. In *The Norton Shakespeare*, New York: WW Norton & Company.

6

PROBLEMATIC SEXUAL EXCESS

In this chapter, I hope to further illuminate the nature of love's impediments by exploring the notion that sexual addictions are a psychopathology of love. The major psychiatric writers on love have not taken up this subject in any depth. This may be a reflection of their limited clinical experience with this group of help seekers and their view that sexual excesses are epiphenomena of remote defects of self-regulation and identity lurking behind their character pathology. This is not an unreasonable general view. Even sexual addiction specialists ultimately reach for earlier experiences that create a negative internalized self-object to explain the behavior.[1]

The concept of character pathology that is invoked in these ideas is much broader than the nine DSM-5's personality disorders. It connotes maladaptive rigidity.

I want to draw attention to three caveats about the character pathology assumption.

The seeming genius of retrospect has its dangers. The view changes when one looks prospectively. A number of population studies have demonstrated that adversities during childhood correlate with poor adult mental health outcomes.[2] The specific form of adult impairment, however, cannot be predicted from the group of specific adversities or any number of adversities.[3] Misfortune or even a specific type of misfortune does not predict depression, addiction, anxiety states, schizophrenia, etc. Retrospective pronouncements about etiology, particularly when they are uttered with authority, are likely to be more limited than we realize. This is one reason why I prefer to work on pathogenesis one step at a time rather than jumping from a phenomenon occurring at age 35 to an explanation that occurred decades ago. Something important—events or processes—might have occurred in between. I must admit, however, that it is difficult when working with some patients not to make such leaps because so many of these men seem to have experienced childhood developmental or family misfortunes and to have had limited opportunities to discuss them at length. I prefer to delineate these processes rather than label their highly individual effects under this familiar rubric.

There is also the problem of diagnostic zeal. In our eagerness to define entities to which we can tag specific treatments, we assume individuals diagnosed with sexual addiction represent a homogeneous group.[4] This was the dominant presumption during the 1980s after Carnes described the pattern.[5] The treatment of sexual addiction was based on a 12-step drug addiction model. When the Internet began to reshape the lives of people, however, pornography addiction quickly became apparent. Much of the early research on men who succumbed to the new easy domestic access to arousing imagery separated those with a substance abuse history from those whose mental health appeared normal until they lost control of themselves. Subsequent reports, both clinical and psychometric, stressed the heterogeneity of these men.[6,7] Along with rise of domestic pornography addiction came respect for the powerful riveting experience of watching attractive young people enjoying sexual activity.[8] The cogent question was how to explain why some merely enjoyed pornography while others could not tear themselves away from it. Character pathology did not seem to answer the question.

Negative countertransference to these patterns is rarely discussed in print, but is easily observed among groups of mental health professionals. Most psychotherapists, particularly women, want nothing to do with these patients. Their behaviors are not the part of the psychopathology universe many therapists wish to visit. When they do deal with them, they prefer to focus on the associated problems—bipolar disorder, for instance, rather than sexual behaviors. I presume from the comments of many trainees and colleagues that the aversion to such cases is based on combinations of disgust, anger, hopelessness, and fear. Many feel that taking a detailed sexual history is an invasion of privacy. The treatment of sexual addiction is often outsourced to specialists. I have wondered whether the assumption of character pathology facilitates the dismissal of these individuals. This is unfortunate because many can benefit from our investment in them.

My previous commitment to study human sexuality in all of its forms enabled me to overcome my negative countertransference in order to work with these men. As a result, I have had the opportunity to watch my notions interact with the dominant thinking about them over many years. Lately I have thought that the heterogeneity of problematic excesses seems to fall into six somewhat overlapping subgroups. A collection of these patients seems to include those who:

1. Have given up on their aspirations to love after divorce, becoming a widower or sensing the impossibility of sexual connection with their wives;
2. Never could tolerate sex in the context of ordinary emotional complexity;
3. Were introduced to pornography before puberty and were so overwhelmed by sexual excitement that their preoccupations interfered with their opportunities to experience an emotionally honest courtship;
4. Possess value systems that view the separation of male recreational sexual behaviors and marital love as natural masculinity;
5. Newly lost their way because the discovery of arousal stimulated by relationshipless sex enhances their boring personal lives; and
6. Have a persistent adolescent erotic obsession that impairs sexual function within an otherwise healthy relationship.

The concept that sexual addiction is a pathology of love is not new. Credit belongs to Carnes, founder of the sexual addiction movement. All six of above subgroups are relevant to the second compendium because they detract from a person's lovability. Number 1 can be found in the third division of the compendium under loss. Numbers 2, 3 and 6 are courtship impediments. Numbers 4 and 5 are captured by character traits that interfere with the ability to behave lovingly. When these patterns are accepted as pathologies of love, clinicians might then ask how they attenuate or destroy love.

Quality of Personal Relationships

The patterns are products of the interplay between an individual's evolving sensibilities and his cultural environment. The stereotypic sexual addict selects sexual relationships that provide no knowledge of the other person. The term love object would not be appropriate for such a partner because the quick accomplishment of genital sex does not generate reciprocal affection or mutual obligation.

Many men with problematic sexual excess patterns understand this and deliberately seek out sex on these terms. Strip clubs, prostitutes, bar pickups, chatting about sex with strangers on the Internet, sex talk for hire by phone, and sexually hooking up with an Internet contact are their usual venues. (Even men who do not partake in these behaviors realize that images of and experiences with relationshipless sex, in certain contexts, will be privately arousing for most of their lives. They have reasons not to participate, however.) These provide just sex.

Others with problematic sexual excesses, however, admit to thinking and feeling love during their sexual behaviors. Some pretend that love exists between the sex worker and themselves. It enhances the experience for them. *I know I am in sexual Disneyland but I don't care, it makes the lap dance more fun. I know she doesn't love me but I pretend she does.* Some imagine love to have begun during the pleasure of a commercial experience. *She was kind, she was into it and I think she really liked me. I want to see her again. Being with her was not anything like being with other hookers. She told me she would be happy if I called again!* These men know that they are playing a private game.

Yet others seem even more desperate to find love in their deteriorated acts. A 30-year-old exhibitionist stalker with a low IQ who privately masturbates wearing panty hose imagines that his teenage victim will love him after he shocks her with his erection. *Yes, I hope that she will come to love me. There is a chance, you know!*

The aspiration to love and be loved is thwarted by many forces. These three examples suggest that when mutual love cannot be attained, the mind may find a way to invent it. The wish to be loved is fundamental to consciousness. There are many ways of creating the illusion of love. When we look closely at those with problematic sexual excesses, we are apt to encounter a few whose needs for the illusion enable us to glimpse the anguish of the loveless.

The Diagnostic Model of Hypersexual Disorder

In 2010, a DSM-5 panel proposed the diagnosis Hypersexual Disorder, attempting to codify clinical knowledge that had been accumulating for three decades. Here is what had been learned. Sexual excesses are destructive to somebody—the patient, the spouse, lover, family, employer, or society.[9] The behaviors may occur at a high frequency or occupy a large amount of time and are expensive in economic, psychological, and social terms. The behaviors may persist despite negative consequences and after the patient states that he wants to stop them. When stopped, they may recur. During the last decade, investigators have objectified the patterns with questionnaires,[10,11] the most recent of which, The Hypersexual Behavior Inventory, closely reflects the proposed diagnostic criteria.[12]

A. Over a period of at least six months, recurrent and intense sexual fantasies, sexual urges, and sexual behavior in association with four or more of the following five criteria:

    (1) Excessive time consumed by sexual fantasies and urges, and by planning for and engaging in sexual behavior.

    (2) Repetitively engaging in these sexual fantasies, urges, and behavior in response to dysphoric mood states (e.g., anxiety, depression, boredom, irritability).

    (3) Repetitively engaging in sexual fantasies, urges, and behavior in response to stressful life events.

    (4) Repetitive but unsuccessful efforts to control or significantly reduce these sexual fantasies, urges, and behavior.

    (5) Repetitively engaging in sexual behavior while disregarding the risk for physical or emotional harm to self or others.

B. Clinically significant personal distress or impairment in social, occupational, or other important areas of functioning associated with the frequency and intensity of these sexual fantasies, urges, and behavior.

C. The sexual fantasies, urges, and behavior are not due to direct physiological effects of exogenous substances (e.g., drugs of abuse or medications) or to Manic Episodes.

D. Age of at least 18 years of age.

The structure of the criteria implies that each element can be answered present or absent by a clinician. Certain phrases are difficult to operationalize, however. For instance, how is a clinician to know what is excessive, intense, or recurrent? Compared to what standard? How is the clinician to judge when the behavior is motivated by dysphoria or stress or when it is motivated by drive, fantasy, opportunity, values, price, etc.? Sexual behavior is often difficult to talk about with mental health professionals. How do we make the judgments required by the criteria when we have an incomplete understanding of the person's life? Wives often send their husbands for treatment of such patterns. The recently caught husband brings the label of sexual addiction from his wife or her therapist. He may be far less distressed by his sexual patterns than by having been discovered by a threatening, suffering, and shocked spouse.

The criteria do not provide guidance on four topics:

1. Orientation. Gay men, on average, have far more sexual partners than their heterosexual counterparts. They have far more casual sexual experiences. They not only have fewer partners to complain about their extra-dyadic behaviors, their relationships are far more often accepting of them. Are clinicians to use the same judgments about the frequency and intensity of urges in hetero- and homosexual groups?
2. Relationship status. Attached and unattached individuals have differing motives for sex.
3. Gender. While all published series of sexual addicts are >90% male, few people think that women are immune to losing control of their sexual behaviors. Their hypersexuality may only involve sex with strangers met in bars or on the Internet, pornography, or masturbation. Clinicians are not used to inquiring about these issues.
4. Paraphilic drivenness. Paraphilias are often present from puberty or before, whereas some men lose self-control only later in life. Estimates of the frequency of paraphilic interests among the hypersexual have ranged between 8 and 33%.[6]

One can be hypersexual and paraphilic, but why is an additional diagnosis necessary. Much has been written in recent years about the difference between a diagnosis' test-retest reliability, validity, and utility.[13,14] Whatever criteria are used to make any behavioral pattern into a psychiatric diagnosis, they had to be approved by at least two separate committees beyond their subsection to become an official disorder. Hypersexual Disorder failed to make the official list published in 2013. The DSM-5 is expected to be an evolving document. The DSM-5 committee did not fund field trials for Hypersexual Disorder but, if new data are gathered that suggest the criteria have validity as well as inter-rater agreement, it may then become an official DSM-5 psychopathology. Whatever these patterns are called—Hypersexual Disorder, Sexual Addiction, Sexual Compulsivity, Sexual Impulsivity, or 17 other names that have been applied over the last 125 years—they have utility for patients, their significant others, and professionals who treat them.[15] Their utility is that the labels generate mental health care, which usually, but not always, is a positive experience and provides hope to the patient and partner.

Currently, however, the high rates of comorbidities involving substance abuse, a mood or anxiety disorder, attention deficit disorder, executive dysfunction, strong narcissistic personality traits in mixed personality disorders, developmental disability, and marital crises make it difficult to have confidence that sexual addiction is the core of the problem. It may be akin to severe insomnia—a problem in itself but also a reflection of some other psychological circumstance. The criticisms of Hypersexual Disorder are reminiscent of those that justified the investment in DSM-5: there is not a clear zone of demarcation between this diagnosis and others.[16] When patients can easily qualify for more than one diagnosis, confidence in the validity of any of them diminishes.

When these criteria were offered to the professional public for comment, negative responses focused on two themes. The first was imprecision and the second was the fear of consequences. The argument was that moral judgments were hidden within the criteria that posed a risk to sexual minorities of being labeled mentally ill. Sexual minorities included those who did not believe in conventional forms of relationships and those whose frequency of sexual behaviors was much higher than average.[17] It may not be possible to discuss any sexual topic without stakeholders expressing worry about the dangers of unexamined assumptions and the diagnosis of the unconventional. Sex and politics are inseparable.

All diagnoses are not created equal. A diagnosis of acute mania, schizophrenia, or autism never ceases to be relevant to clinical work with the patient even when an acute episode is resolved. Many other diagnoses are relevant for only a short time. Many sexual diagnoses fade in importance as we try to understand what created the problem. The criteria of Hypersexual Disorder imply that the pattern is a coping mechanism for stress or dysphoria. This is reasonable for some cases, but I don't think the writers imagined that the stress could have been failure to establish or maintain a loving bond. The proposed criteria for Hypersexual Disorder illustrate how far away from the concept of love and its impediments we have gone.

Nosology is just categorization of the range of mental disturbances. It does not suggest pathogenesis or treatment, which are the primary responsibilities of clinicians. Diagnosis is the first step to treatment, but it often turns out to be a perfunctory one.

Subtle Ways Problematic Sexual Excesses Impede Loving

Many of these patterns impede loving in ways that are not subtle. Before partner discovery occurs, the man's time, energy, and interest are elsewhere. The partner usually notes this but explains it away, with or without his help. The man is hiding, often dishonest, and typically has less sexual interest in the partner. When confronted by his pornography use in the home, he may normalize it or get angry over the concern and blame it on the partner's sexual unavailability. Blaming the partner, minimizing one's involvement, having secret activities, and emotional withdrawal all come into a new perspective upon discovery and produce his partner's rage, alienation, and the realization that "I am unable to love him." While the discovery of the pattern precipitates the decision to end the relationship for many, for many others it creates a decision to withdraw interest, caring, optimism, and sexual desire and the recognition that he will not be the source of much pleasure in the future. Relationships then become loveless endurance tests.

One subtle way excesses impede loving can be seen in some clinicians' ideas about a defect that underlies the loss of sexual self-control—a poor capacity to relate intimately to others.[18] This is obvious in many men whose incapacities limit courtship success. Clinicians see more subtle forms of such incapacity after a relationship is established.

After the crisis of discovery has abated, and the couple persists in treatment in order to reactivate their sexual life together, a familiar pattern emerges. When the partner is again receptive to sexual bonding, the men, despite what they say, are not. They display the iconic psychopathology of love described in Chapter Three. They cannot integrate affection and sexual pleasure in the same person. These men emphatically state that they love their partners and desire to continue the relationship. They are now much more involved in the partner's and the children's lives, but their love does not include a sexual component. Here are a few examples.

Adam, the 84-year-old icon: A healthy, semi-retired successful investor, married to his second wife for 34 years, had a normal sexually active courtship with both of his wives until he lost his interest within weeks following his weddings. Numerous therapists armed with different techniques and ideologies have failed to get him to engage in genital activity a second time after one of the experiences that he dreads. Never potent with his wives, he has been having intercourse with or receiving fellatio from prostitutes since he was 18 years old. He estimates his lifelong average is weekly. It has been only in the last five years that has he felt the need to ensure his potency with a medication.

His first wife divorced him after twenty-five childless, sexless years. His second wife, decades younger, provided a ready-made family, which kept them busy avoiding focusing on their asexual life. Now that the children have their separate lives, she has come to the painful understanding that sex will never happen between them. For almost thirty years, she was unaware of his prostitute habit and coped with the problem with her own excesses. But since she discovered "his addiction," he has promised her to give up massage parlors at least three times and subsequently was found out. He has no sexual interest in any sexual behaviors with anyone other than a prostitute. His wife says he has interest only in himself, money, and politics. She often laments, "What about me? I feel so alone with you!" He repeats that he loves her.

Ben acts out. Forty years of "ridiculous" behaviors began with the discovery of his father's porn collection of she-males. This induced an aroused fascination with feminized males (well developed breasts and erections) that was admixed over the years with strip clubs, prostitutes, penetration of, and by, and fellatio of she-males, ads for sexual adventures, masturbation at work to porn and other ways of having a secret life. He discovered at age 22 that he was the son of swingers when he happened upon pictures taken by his father of his naked mother in various sex acts with men.

Individual, group, and couples therapy enabled Ben to recognize the triggers and the personal consequences of his acting out. After two years of work, he was able to stop and to deal more genuinely with his wife. It was always apparent that Ben, who describes himself as a very strange heterosexual, wanted to make love with his wife but could not generate the motivation to do so. Exhaustion, headaches, and arguments were eventually recognized as his avoidance mechanisms and were overcome. He says that what he has done sexually has made him undeserving of sex with his wife. "I hate myself for what I have done. I am so ashamed," Ben lamented. Her invitations are rarely accepted because he fears the inability to maintain an erection. The couple credits therapy for much improvement in their lives. He talks more. He said somewhat proudly, "I know more about what I feel now." We thought that they had overcome the problem when they had three lovely intercourse experiences in a month, but sexual avoidance returned. His wife has become a paranoid vigilant monitor of his daily movements and expenditures. This creates bickering, which diminishes the likelihood of sex. Ben frequently reaffirms his love for his wife and their children. She has come close to ending the marriage many times, but it is apparent to her that they both love each other deeply. "Sexually I am a basket case, but don't give up on me," he pleaded.

Charles has a maladaptive obsession: Fifty years old, he has had the same erotic ideal since he began masturbation at around 14 years of age. Twenty-five years ago, he quickly fell in love with a secretary who had his dream body type: a small waist, muscular buttocks. When I met the couple after 20 years of marriage, she had had a long-standing severe treatment-resistant depression that she blamed on his porn addiction. He spoke of his frustration in having such a beautiful wife who refused sex and was a dysfunctional mother and wife. Eventually, his long suffering gave way to a decision to end the marriage. Several guilt-ridden years later, he fell in love with a highly functional, independent, happy, beautiful, sexually eager loving woman with no children. All of this is perfect; my kids love her. She is a dream come true except that she does not have a thin waist. She is not fat. She is in great shape. From the beginning of their physical intimacies, his potency was inconstant. He thinks his aversion to her midsection is the reason for his intermittent potency. As I listen to this very accomplished man ruminate about this, I am transported to my early adolescence when a girl's shape seemed more important to me than her being. Charles is quite civilized and mature in other respects, but he cannot subjectively fully accept his fiancée.[19] He often looks frightened and says, "You got to fix me."

His pornography use has dwindled from almost daily during marriage to weekly when his fiancée is not present, but his erotic aesthetics have not changed. My clarifications seem reasonable to us but after a year of trying, there is still no cause for celebration. As wonderful a story as his courtship has been, his erotic obsession is foreboding, He is

74

embarrassed that his adolescent sensibility lives on untouched by experience. Of course, I have wondered what woman possessed a thin waist from his past. His answer: "My mother was heavy-set. I think I just always liked women of that size and shape—it is what is attractive to me."

Charles regularly raves about having the domestic bliss that he used to long for in marriage. His fiancée's responses to his inability to sustain an erection are ideal. She is so easy going; she does not pressure me. She seems so happy to have any kind of sex. Nonetheless, a thin-waisted new employee recently created a great temptation for him. "I know I won't do it, but I think about it all the time." I wonder whether Charles' erotic obsession will eventually render this couple as relatively asexual.

As an aside, I recently watched a separated man give up a loving wife who was "perfect" except for the wide hips that sexually turned him off. He had never been faithful to his wife whom he "respects and loves dearly."

Of course, these three men have backstories that are not presented in the sketches. Adam felt his mother so repeatedly disappointed him that as a child he vowed never to allow himself to depend on another woman again. He has been loyal to that pledge. When individuals fall in love and stay in love, each person's sense of self involves the other. This is starkly illustrated upon the death of a beloved partner: I buried part of myself today. In public, Adam behaves reasonably well, but when he is alone with his wife, his behavior is often affectively empty. I can feel this in conjoint sessions—ignoring her comments, not grasping exactly what she is saying, not feeling her feelings. She has long felt this deficiency of connection but has not been able to find the words to describe it. You bastard! does not quite capture the lack of empathic caring.

Ben hated his father's expectations for him to be his clone. He hated his mother's mindless obedience to her dictator. He found it difficult to share his family's sexual unconventionalities with me. It seemed obvious that some of the triggers for his sudden impulses for unconventional sex were his father's behavior towards him. When he joked that his parents were a piece of work or that his dad was a character, he was relatively inarticulate in explaining how. The extent of his rage, always mixed with resignation, only gradually became apparent to him as more stories were conveyed: his discoveries of trans-porn and pictures of his mother with other men. Ben's expressions of love were impeded by his full knowledge of his secret behavior and his guilt. They were both ego-syntonic and ego-dystonic. Ben's loving behaviors were limited by shame and defensive hostility. Unlike Adam, however, I could feel his respect, affection, and empathy for his wife. He particularly enjoyed her characterizations of her in-laws because she was both more articulate and observant, but also more hostile.

Charles was informed that his mother was mentally ill when he was around 10 and her hospitalizations began. As she slowly recovered, he felt himself growing hungry for attention and caring. He coped with this emptiness by taking pride in his responsibility. He devoted himself to proving that he was capable as a solo agent. To this day, he is still proving that his family's adversity will not limit him. When he is embarrassed to ask his fiancée for just fellatio, it seems to me that expression of attentive devotion to him is too much to ask for. He seems to want nurturance but is not able to share this with her. He says that it is like he is a little kid. "Yes," I say, "and what is wrong with that?"

When I was a younger psychiatrist, I thought that my unfolding awareness of a person's dynamics would catalyze behavioral change. Adam, Ben, Charles, and I are still working on it. Working on pathogenesis is humbling. It should be. We are multidetermined and many of our behavioral patterns only slowly evolve, with or without therapy. There is, after all, a prodigious mystery called maturation. When problematic sexual excess was labeled an addiction in the 1980s, one of the compelling reasons for the term was the frequency of relapse.[20] Sexual tendencies do not disappear. They recede. In the case of destructive sexual impulses, they are deliberately fought against. Hopefully maturation, time, or assisted understanding weakens the impulses a bit. These same three elements may also improve the capacity to suppress and to sublimate.

Misdiagnosis by a Spouse

Two miseries are inherent in the discovery of a partner's secret sexual life: a sense of betrayal and having been a trusting fool. The crisis of discovery unleashes a torrent of feelings and a profound sense of uncertainty. When a partner is enraged over an affair, it is often described as sordid. Problematic sexual excesses are also morally distasteful and contemptuous to the partner, but they carry an additional burden—he is a far less substantial a person than I thought.

While therapists may not be able to agree on what exactly qualifies a person for membership in the sexual addiction universe, we sometimes can quickly recognize when a person fails to qualify. In these circumstances, the therapist can turn a spouse's horror into only an embarrassment.

Douglas is innocent. While her schizophrenic mother was slowly dying of pancreatic cancer, an exhausted preoccupied college professor discovered her quiet, quality control official husband looking at adult heterosexual pornography on his computer. Shocked by this discovery, she threatened to divorce him for his infidelity. At the next weekly session with her therapist, he suggested that her husband was likely a sexual addict who needed help. When I saw Douglas, he was befuddled by her intense reaction and her disbelief of his explanation. He described himself to be "a nervous wreck, unable to sleep and eat." He hesitantly asked, Was I unfaithful?

The facts seemed to be that her discovery of him masturbating to a computer video of a couple having oral and penile-vaginal intercourse was the second incident in a two month period. He and his wife reported a mutually satisfying sexual relationship for 38 years, which had recently become less frequent because of her fatigue from her obligations to her mother. Her mother had long been a significant burden to both of them. He had no other extra dyadic sexual behaviors or interests. The couple handled the funeral in their typical cooperative fashion. At a conjoint session soon thereafter, I explained his behavior more benignly. She quickly abandoned her diagnosis and apologized. He quickly forgave. Each was relieved, both because their ordeal was finally over and because there was no reason for this loving couple to separate.

Love, Paraphilia, and Problematic Sexual Excess

When paraphilic problematic sexual excesses preclude pair bonding, the problem reverberates within the man, his victim, a sex worker, and his family of origin, if they know about it at all. It is quite different within couples. The problematic excess may be contained within their union through partner sex and solitary masturbation or it may generate infidelity. The latter group presents in crisis with the shock of infidelity and the sense that "my partner is sick," meaning he is far less than I had judged him to be. He is paying a dominatrix to beat him and command him to serve her! What! Who is this man? How come I did not know about this about him? I don't know what to do. The man I have loved is not the man I knew.

The group that contains the paraphilia within the marriage illustrates love and its compromises. Containing the paraphilia within the home is what some partners do for love. The partner's attitude toward the man's sexual requirement is the key to whether the paraphilia diminishes the capacity to love. The paraphilic's gratitude for the partner's indulgence may generate demonstrative moments of affection, interest, caring, and optimism on his part. Paraphilia is created by and for the man. It cannot engage the partner to the same degree. It is an act of love to play the game. Stories of partners' acceptances of the requirements are very lovely, but clinicians also learn of the story with the partner's attitude changes. The paraphilic may feel betrayed. You bought the idea when we met and now you are withdrawing from our deal. That is not fair to me! The needs of the man and the needs of the partner collide. The reaffirmation of the bond, the reinforcement of each partner's gender identity, the attenuation of small resentments, and the diminished frequency of thought of other sexual partners—all of which are facilitated by mutually satisfying lovemaking—disappear as the sexual nurturant system vanishes from their lives. This has consequences.

Evan was happy for a long time. When they courted and during the early years of marriage, he and his future wife seemed to be quite happy together. Children took their energies for a long period, but when they agreed to increase the frequency of sex, Evan began to have potency problems. Evan eventually told her about his secret clothing fetish and how it began. When he unexpectedly had to sleep over an aunt's house in 5th grade, in a silly mood she gave him a slip to wear. They pretended they were girls and then slept together in a double bed, both wearing full-length slips. Since, the memory of that evening has excited him. There was no sexual behavior, per se, between them. In adolescence he masturbated wearing a slip, loving the sensation of silk and began pretending to be a woman. He discovered a trove of transvestite stories and kept them stashed away. He confessed to his wife that he would like to put on her slip as a prelude to lovemaking. He wanted just to lie in bed with her wearing identical slips for a few moments each time. (He did not at that point tell her that he had been wearing her slip to masturbate.) She agreed, his potency was instantly restored and for most of the next twenty years, he pretended they were two ladies sleeping together. She endured the game because it guaranteed his erection and energized his interest in her. They conceived their third child this way. Over time, however, she tired of the pattern, felt increasingly insulted by his requirement and one day when he asked to play the game after a long layoff, she became overcome with affect and blurted out that she wanted to make love with a man who liked being man. Although this pleasant gentle man was in psychotherapy for dysthymia, he did not share his secret there. When they sought help for erection problems in their 26th year of marriage, they could not tell me this history until the third conjoint session. True to their history, once our work started, they returned to the ritual and he was happy. When he tried to get by with only the fantasy, each was dissatisfied. He could not sustain arousal without the feel of the slip. She found him emotionally absent and his touch mechanical. She apologized for her withdrawal, but said that she simply could not do this anymore. "It depresses me too much. I need a man who wants me. I'm not some old lady, and I don't want to have sex with one. I don't even wear slips like that anymore."

She eventually decided to divorce. She met with another woman through the Internet who said that she didn't mind a little erotic game. He was pleased that she knew that everyone has quirks. Evan moved to another state to live with her. His wife sunk deeper into depression.

Alternative Concepts of Masculinity

Pornography, gentlemen's clubs, escort services, prostitution, erotic Internet games, sex chat lines, etc. are well-established businesses that are integrated into culture. It would surprise few people to learn that varieties of these commercial operations exist even in regions where they are prohibited by law. Some men grow through adolescence and adulthood partaking in these offerings and experience them as valuable in meeting their needs for sexual experience, male socialization, and stabilizing their gender identities. They call it fun. Clinicians who do not share these experiences and sensibilities may initially experience such expressions as rationalizations of pathological behaviors. Yet, in taking care of men, one can easily develop uneasiness about some of our own thinking. Where is the line to be drawn between the normal and abnormal sexual interests of straight and sexual minority men? By what method are we to determine its location? Intuition? Identification with the partner?

There are heterosexuals whose values or sensibilities support the ambition that after marriage they will have two venues of sex. The most important will be the sex that promotes family formation, relationship maintenance, and marital love. These men expect their marital sexual behaviors to become less exciting with time, complicated by life, marital politics, and menstruation. They are not shocked that sex becomes familiar, routine, and a bit boring. They expect that the least important venue will be the most exciting. The venue is in meaningless, relationless behaviors. Such men know, of course, to keep their beliefs and behaviors from their wives. Their extramarital activities are well known to their friends who loyally keep their secrets. This is culturally supported to different degrees in different countries.

One might be tempted to refer to these lives as aberrations due to character pathology. I prefer to consider them as reflecting different assumptions about what love requires of a man. A person's understanding of what love requires can change in response to many events, including a partner's distress.

Frank's alternate form of masturbation. A happily married stockbroker, a father of three children, was discovered by his wife to have purchased "sensual massages" monthly for years along with his more frequent standard massages. His satisfying twice-weekly marital sexual life was also secretly supplemented by masturbation to pornography several times per week. At least four times a year he visited a strip club with customers, cousins, or friends. He considered himself faithful because he never engaged in intercourse. He viewed his massages with "happy endings" as a variant of masturbation. His wife had often commented to him that he always thought of himself first and always found a way to do what he wanted. Frank was shocked by his wife's profound distress. He had known to keep his activity secret because she would not approve, but he had no idea how depressed she would become. In therapy he developed a surge of understanding of her viewpoint. He began to view his sexual pursuits as immature and self-centered. I graduated college ten years ago, but I am acting like time stood still. He committed himself to growing up. He and his wife began having more sex and he invested himself in understanding the waves of distress his wife felt for four months after her discovery. Masturbation ceased.

Frank proved to be a grateful good student. His shock reflected, I told him, his deficient understanding of his wife's internal life. He needed to develop a sustained interest in her perceptions, a continuing awareness of her feelings, and an appreciation of the values her devotion to the family rested upon. She would not be able to continue to love him fully if he continued thinking of her as a handmaiden who served his conventional needs but then could be dismissed so he could pursue his others pleasures. I suggested that he consider adopting the goal "to have her fully love you when you when your children are out of the house." I apologized once to him for talking so much during the session. He said, Please don't stop, I really am learning a lot from you. I wish I came here before.

Don't I wish all such men were as receptive as Frank. I was unable to influence Gregory, a man twenty years older than Frank.

Gregory runs a successful tower construction business in several states. He and his crew are gone several nights a week most weeks. Gregory not only sells the jobs, he supervises their construction and provides skilled labor as needed. His wife of thirty years, now a chronically hypomanic devoted church volunteer, thinks he is a sex addict and alcoholic (he has had three DUIs). He claims that he is faithful because he has never had sex with another woman. He often has sex with his wife after his nights out at strip clubs when he is in town. He does not consider himself to be an alcoholic or a sex addict nor does he agree that his wife is mentally ill; she is just a bit eccentric. Everyone in my business does this. What is the big deal? This works for me, this brings in money for us. What am I supposed to do nights that I am away? Read books! Come on, I like to drink, we all do. I bet you do, too.

The more fuss his wife made about his need for treatment, the more insincere his participation became. "My kids are grown, it's time to enjoy myself. I enjoy my life. Nobody's going to tell me what I like," Gregory says. I ask about his DUIs. "I have learned my lesson," he explains. "When I have had too much to drink, someone else drives." When I repeated his wife's claims that he often staggers when he comes home, he responded, " Have you noticed that she exaggerates everything?"

I never spoke of love to Gregory.

Problematic conventional sexual excess can occur within marriage.

References

1 Collins, G.N., & Adelman, A. (2011). *Breaking the cycle: Free yourself from sex addiction, porn addiction and shame.* Oakland, CA: New Harbinger Publications.
2 McLaughlin, K.A., Grief-Green, J., Gruber, M.J., Sampson N.A., Zaslavsky, A.M., & Kessler, R.C.G. (2012). Childhood adversities and first onset of psychiatric disorders in a national sample of US adolescents. *Archives of General Psychiatry, 69*(11), 1151–60.
3 Pietrek, C., Elbert, T., Weierstall, R., Müller, O., & Rockstroh, B. (2012). Childhood adversities in relation to psychiatric disorders. *Psychiatry Research, epub,* (12), 696–8.
4 Cantor, J.M., Klein, C., Lykins, A., Rullo, J.E., Thaler, L., & Walling, B.R. (2013, 2 March). A treatment oriented typology of self-identified hypersexuality referrals. *Archives of Sexual Behavior epublication.*
5 Carnes, P. (2002). *Don't call it love.* New York: Bantam Books.
6 Kaplan, M., & Kreuger, R. (2010). Diagnosis, assessment, and treatment of hypersexuality. *Journal of Sexual Research, 47*, 181–198.
7 Reid, R. (2009). Exploring relationships of psychopathology in hypersexual patients using the MMPI-2. *Journal of Sex and Marital Therapy, 35*(4), 294–310.
8 Cooper, A. (2000). *Cybersex and sexual compulsivity: The dark side of the force.* New York: Taylor and Frances.

9 Goodman, A. (2001). What is in a name? Terminology for designating a syndrome driven by sexual behavior. *Sexual Addiction and Compulsivity*, 8, 191–213.

10 Kalichman, S. C., & Rompa, D. (2001). The sexual compulsivity scale: Further development and use with HIV-positive persons. *Journal of Personality Assessment*, 76(3), 379–395.

11 Minor, M., Coleman, E., Center, B., Ross, M., & Rosser, B. R. S. (2007). The compulsive sexual behaviors inventory: Psychometric properties. *Archives of Sexual Behavior*, 36, 579–587.

12 Reid, R., Garos, S., & Carpenter, B. N. (2011). Reliability, validity, and psychometric properties of the hypersexual behavioral inventory in a outpatient sample of men. *Sexual Addiction and Compulsivity*, 18, 30–51.

13 Kraemer, H. (2013). Validity and psychiatric diagnosis. *JAMA Psychiatry*, 70(2), 138–139.

14 Kendell, R. (2003). Distinguishing between the validity and utility of psychiatric diagnoses. *American Journal of Psychiatry*, 160(1), 4–12.

15 Levine, S. (2012). Review: Problematic sexual excesses. *Neuropsychiatry*, 2(1), 69–79.

16 Kupfer, D., & Regier, D. (2011). Neuroscience, clinical evidence, and the future of psychiatric classification in DSM-5. *American Journal of Psychiatry*, 168(7), 672–674.

17 Walters, G., Knight, R. A., & Langstrom, N. (2011). Is hypersexuality dimensional? Evidence for the DSM-5 from general population and clinical samples. *Archives of Sexual Behavior*, 4(6), 1309–1321.

18 Marcus, I. (2010). Men who lose control over their sexual behavior. In SB Levine, CB Risen, SA Althof (eds.) *Handbook of clinical sexuality for mental health professionals* (2nd ed., pp. 267–290). New York: Routledge.

19 Freud, S. (1912). On the universal tendency to debasement in the sphere of love. In S. Freud, *The standard edition of the complete psychological works of Sigmund Freud* (Vol. XI, pp. 177–190). London: Hogarth Press.

20 Carnes, P. (2001). *Out of the shadows: Understanding sexual addiction.* City Center, Minn.: Hazelden.

7

INFIDELITY

Infidelities exist on a spectrum ranging from the problematic sexual excesses to affairs of the heart. Most instances of infidelity are located between these two poles. Betrayal of the expectation for monogamy, which by definition is infidelity, creates its own unavoidable psychology for the unfaithful and their two partners. Monogamy does not guarantee mental health, but it is a protective factor against significant adversities. The unfaithful and their families are a discovery away from crisis.

The expectation for monogamy has been socially constructed over the previous four centuries.[1] Its adaptive advantages are rarely stated, but when they are, it is easier to grasp the reasons for hesitance to be unfaithful and for the emotional disturbances that it can induce. Monogamy helps:

To preserve the couple's mental, physical, social, and economic health;
To preserve the structure of family in order to facilitate children's emotional development;
To preserve the continuity of relationships with parents, siblings, extended family, and friends; and
To prevent destructive cynicism about the possibility of marital or relationship happiness in all concerned.

This might be simply summarized by saying that the institution and maintenance of monogamy is protective of family structure.

Returning to One End of the Spectrum

In the previous chapter, I illustrated some of the ways that men with problematic sexual excess limit their capacities to love and to be loved. Some excesses are more destructive to love than others. Frequent use of prostitutes, for instance, is usually more offensive to a partner than is frequent masturbation to pornography. Homosexual encounters have different meanings than opposite sex ones. The discovery of any set of these excesses may precipitate divorce when it is experienced as the last straw in an already compromised interpersonal situation. Beyond betrayal itself, these patterns create the impediments to loving through five related behavior pathways: dishonesty, emotional inscrutability, irritability, limited sexual interest, and physical unavailability. Often lurking behind the problematic sex and these challenging behaviors is the man's inability to sustain a caring bond. Experience with the latter over long periods of time is what often enables the partner to declare the betrayal to be the last straw. An extramarital reflection of the inability to care for or invest in another appears at the end of an involvement with a lengthy opportunistic noncommercial sexual relationship. The man feels relief rather than grief. The absence of grief is the telltale indicator of his unwillingness or inability to invest in a partner beyond sex.

An exception to this pattern leads us to a major concept about love. Two individuals in an extramarital relationship of convenience, so called sex buddies, can be surprised by the unintended powerful loving bond that gradually creeps upon them from repeated sexual intimacies. What begins as just sex in a larger pattern of problematic sexual excess transforms into something more caring and enduring. The clandestine couple becomes trapped in the web of their desire for more than sex. The processes of love begin to occur—increased knowledge of one another, friendship, and deeper attachment. Love conveys hope, however it gets started. This outcome among some men who are labeled sexual addicts reminds us that sex and love are both governed by their dynamic malleable natures, not by our theories. Our concepts about sex and love chase after the phenomena in order to better understand them. There are reasons that we can never be too certain about the appearance and disappearances of love. We are too often surprised by what happens to be authoritative about these topics.

Affairs of the Heart

Affairs of the heart, love affairs, are a qualitatively different form of infidelity than those that are associated with sexual excesses. These affairs form in admiration and respect, grow into friendship and evolve into early passionate sexualized attachment. They then evolve in their unique ways determined by the psychological and social circumstances of each person. I have witnessed three categories of outcomes.

The affair remains undiscovered

and continues to satisfy both participants for a long period of time, occasionally until death.

and continues to satisfy both until one person's psychological or social circumstances create a sputtering end that is difficult for each person.

but creates changes within the marriage that

deteriorate it by the increase in complaints to, and about, the unaware spouse.

are misattributed by the spouse to some other factor.

but creates a dishonestly explained separation in a marriage due to pressure from the lover.

The affair is discovered

and ends.

and precipitates divorce but does not lead to marriage with the lover.

and precipitates divorce and marriage to the lover.

The affair creates an additional crisis, such as

a pregnancy.

a major depression or bout of substance abuse in one of the three key individuals or their children.

a suicide attempt in one of their families.

Our clinical observations about affairs of the heart are important. They are limited, however, because they develop during the crises of discovery. The perspective of the aggrieved partner and the person having the affair prior to discovery typically inform our views. The views of the paramour rarely make their way into professional publications and discourse. Clinical observations do not have the larger scope that novels, movies, and television depictions of love affairs occasionally have. They may not even reflect what we know from our own lives. We tend to create retrospective accounts of why an affair was undertaken by focusing on the defects of the errant spouse or the justifications of the unfaithful spouse.

The natural history of affairs of the heart includes their psychologies of formation, evolution, dissolution, and later repercussions. Even the marvelous classic cultural resources for understanding love affairs such as, Tolstoy's *Anna Karenina* leave one to wonder about one or more of these processes. Psychiatric writings that invoke works of fiction tend to well describe transient affective aspects of the complex experience.[2]

There are three dramatis personae in the triangular crises of heterosexual affairs. We rarely see all of the individuals involved in the drama but we hear of them from our patient. When our patient is a couple who is trying to preserve their marriage, the third person is typically initially viewed with derision by the aggrieved spouse. This allows some of the anger at the spouse to be deflected to the paramour. A scapegoat is created and viewed as a morally defective invader of the sanctity of the marriage. Of course, the partner was not the victim; he or she made the many necessary decisions along the way. However wise or unwise those decisions might ultimately prove to be, the partner was an equal participant. Scapegoating provides the aggrieved with a modicum of temporary comfort to consider that the spouse was seduced by this evil person. Eventually, spouses turn their attention to the partner's decisions.

In this chapter, our interest in love affairs is in the love that is experienced. There is a central question in these crises that requires courage for the aggrieved to ask and requires wisdom for the partner to answer. *Do you love her (him)?* The correct answer, *Of course,* is usually evident to the one who is having the affair. This answer often is not what is said. At this dramatic moment, the multiple meanings of love come into play—Ambition? Attachment? Moral obligation? Management process? Emotion? Illusion?[3] Clinicians can appreciate the value of not being able to define what one feels in a way that another can understand, the value of not being able to describe the personal transformations that a new intimacy has created, and the value of the artful dodge.

The spouse wants the answer to be: *No, not really* and will sometimes accept a vague meandering answer topped off with, *I don't really know what love is.* Love is, after all, an elusive abstract concept. The partner has felt wonderful with the paramour—understood, valued, alive, and eager for another meeting. The sex was usually vibrant, and the pleasures of their evolving union created a deeply caring connection. In the person's mind, this is love, as good as it gets, and what has not been experienced for a very long time with the spouse. But, it feels so dangerous to share that with the aggrieved person. *Haven't I done enough damage already?*

Welcome to paradox. Where does wisdom lie? *Yes, I love the person* allows for honest forthright discussion of the dual predicaments that now exist with the spouse and paramour, but it causes immediate hopelessness and anger in the spouse and may trigger a separation or divorce, an outcome that may not yet be desired. *No, I do not love the person* makes the spouse wonder about the mate's pro-miscuous nature but runs the greater risk of not being believed. The perception of the lie may make the spouse immediately feel hopeless and angry and may trigger a separation or divorce. If a therapist is in the room, four eyes look intensely at the professional for guidance. The dodge often takes the form of *I am not sure.* At this moment, the partner's uncertainty provides the aggrieved spouse with a smidgen of hope.

Like chess players who anticipate several next moves, some aggrieved spouses foresee the danger and uncertainties of the answer to *Do you love him (her)?* They do not directly ask the question or, if they do, do not wait for an answer. When they ask and the answer is *Yes,* however, a new set of possibilities comes into focus. This is the moment when the therapist can be particularly valuable. The loving attachment is acknowledged, the reasons for staying together are summa-rized, the separate unilateral processes of grief for each of them are highlighted, and the aggrieved spouse is counseled against harsh ultimatums.

We don't expect the aggrieved spouse to feel sorry for the partner's loss of ac-cess to his or her lover, but we don't want to pretend that a new love lost can never be thought about again. We do expect the partner to take a new great interest in the mental processes of the aggrieved spouse. This will feel like caring to the aggrieved. It conveys hope because it actually creates psychological intimacy between them. The errant partner gains from this as well. He or she is often astounded and frightened by the recurrent intensities of distress in the spouse and comes to realize the destructiveness of the extramarital pleasures. The aggrieved spouse's suffering often triggers the realization that the spouse is still actually loved. Then the question *To whom do I owe my greater allegiance, spouse or paramour* comes into clear focus.

No affair of the heart is simple or without ambivalence. The aggrieved spouse wants to rely on the ambivalence as a means of maintaining the marriage and may offer some of these thoughts: *It really wasn't a good idea. It would not have worked out well. Everyone is on their best behavior at the beginning. You would have been burdened by the aftermath of divorce. Your kids would hate you. Real life is more than sneaking off to have sex. We can't afford a divorce. You would have eventually been unhappy in that relationship, too.* These ideas would naturally occur in time to the errant spouse, but before they can be internally processed and acknowledged as realistic considerations, grief, longing, and memories of delight prevail. Ending an affair is not just a matter of logic and practicality.

When the aggrieved spouse says, *You must never see or talk to that person again!* I gently intervene. I remark that such an order has a high risk of backfiring because it does not take into account the need for lovers to be together. It is a set up for further dishonesty. I suggest that the couple equally acknowledge the emotional realities and unrealities of early love. Falling in love is part imagination, and its joys are usually accompanied by a conscious unspoken concern about whether this venture is a good idea. The couple also needs to acknowledge the frightening realities of abandonment and familial restructuring, including the division of assets. I sometimes think that the most important thing that I say in these heated moments is the statement of the goal to balance these temporary forces in their lives with discussion and respect for each other's plight. Crises do not last forever. Passions and the meanings that underlie them evolve. I must admit, however, that I am never certain what a member of the couple hears or remembers of what I say.

Henry's calm, pleasant, unemotional happy life changed into the pain of betrayal and the humiliation of failing as a husband in an instant. Henry had trusted Janice implicitly despite the fact that he perceived that they never fully clicked sexually. Janice never complained about their sexual life. They were devoted parents, had many friends and had cordial relationships with their families. Her athletic skills progressed rapidly under the guidance of an instructor, who also taught her son. Their six-month friendship was transformed by the coach's declaration that he wanted to kiss her. During the preceding months, Janice began to think that her husband was preoccupied with his career and seemed distant from her. After her next lesson, she said, "Just this once." This gradually led to sexual intercourse within two weeks. Janice was astounded by how exciting the new sexual behavior proved to be; it was much more compelling than her quieter, 4–6 times per month, regularly orgasmic sexual life with Henry. Until then, he had been her only sexual partner. Guilt led her to end the relationship after four months, but she quickly resumed for another seven months. The lovers had no interest in leaving their families, never said they loved each other, did not talk much in person, and did not complain to one another about their marriages. They communicated by texting, saw each other several times a week, and had intercourse weekly. Henry noticed that Janice was spending a lot more time away from him in their home. After he dreamt that she was having an affair, he checked her cell phone records and confronted her. She immediately cried in grave shameful embarrassment, promised to end the relationship and said that she wanted to stay married. When asked, she claimed she did not love the coach. She apologized repeatedly. She thought that no one else knew about the relationship. The couple agreed to tell no one about this. The next day Henry visited the coach who corroborated Janice's story, apologized, agreed not contact her again, and pleaded with Henry not to tell his wife.

When I saw them together, Henry was the most distressed person in the room. He said he was devastated, could not sleep or eat, had anxiety all day long, and felt pressure in his chest. After a month of individual and conjoint sessions, Henry decided he would remain married to Janice. He emphasized that he clearly was, by far, the better man. He felt he understood as much as could be understood about what happened. He was convinced that *Janice truly loves me* and was getting over the other man. *She made a very big mistake in judgment to get involved.*

He was able to have sex again on day 11. Their sexual behavior began to have an intensity never previously felt by them.

In this first month I was consistently interested in each of their viewpoints, concerns, and wishes for the future. Henry remained uncommitted about how things would work out until Janice patiently answered all his questions and maintained a consistent concern about his recurring emotional breakdowns. Initially, he could not understand how she could love him and sleep with another man. Then, *If you did not love him, how could you have had sex with him?* He could not grasp why she did not agree that it was a poor idea to continue to take their son for lessons from that coach. As life was settling back to normal, Henry expressed his concern that Janice seemed too ready to sweep the affair under the rug. She did not want him to mention it. I gave him an analogy to coping with cancer chemotherapy: both partners are suffering anxieties but choose to lighten each other's burden by not fully discussing their subjective experience. Another calm week occurred complete with weekend lovemaking. Each was busy with their usual tasks. He said the cancer analogy helped him protect her from his deepest worries. Henry felt that Janice was putting 100% of herself into him and the children again. He worried the affair was a response to a problem that she felt in the relationship that in the future might cause trouble. He feared *that the shadow of another person would now always be intoxicating to her.* Janice worried about the meaning of always having to initiate their sexual opportunities. *Yes, but once you do, everything flows normally and we are both pleased. But why won't you initiate it?* He could not exactly say what he knew: *I adapted to your dislike of sex and did not ever want to force it on you.* That evening, Henry was very sad, had difficulty sleeping, and felt that Janice wanted sexual things from him that he could not provide. *I only want you to indicate that you really want me sexually!* They had a long talk. He awakened in the morning feeling better, but now she was sad, worried, and confused. *I thought we had made progress but last night you were like you were a while ago.* They went away together for her athletic event and had the best sex of their lives. After the competition, she tearfully told him how grateful she was for his support that weekend, meaning as well, during the trying previous six weeks. Henry was pleased. They had marvelous sex again before they returned home.

Henry's mental state during these weeks of evolving crisis was typical of the betrayed person. He was struggling to find answers to four questions. The swirl of these questions and his incomplete answers makes individuals feel like they are "going crazy."[4]

1. What is the personal meaning of the infidelity to me?
2. What is the best way I can respond to it?
3. Will I be abandoned?
4. Why did this happen?

I listened to Henry struggle with these questions. At times, I rephrased his concerns in terms of a specific question. Various affects accompanied his questions, of course, and I made sure that he labeled them accurately. I did this with him in a calm, relaxed fashion, gently repeating that the answers to the questions and his feelings will evolve. When he asked in Janice's presence, *Does anyone ever get over this? Will I be able to trust her again?* I explained that the Chinese write the character for crisis by combining the words danger and opportunity. I had seen that they were in grave danger. I was there to help them work through the danger in order to create a better life of their choosing. I asserted that many people get over a spouse's affair, but that I did not want to mislead them into thinking that there was no possibility of future unhappiness. Why would anyone aspire to forget that an affair occurred? I asked rhetorically. I told them that I often dramatically pointed to my patients and accused them of being meaning makers. *Janice's affair has different meanings to each of you. We all should act as though we know that over time meanings change, behaviors are viewed from a different perspective, and that which is painful can sometimes eventually become discussed more lightly. I neither want to trivialize what had happened nor do I want to regard this as the worst possible thing that can happen in life.*

Janice's experience was also typical in many ways. Five questions usually preoccupy the conversations in individual therapy with the unfaithful partner. Some of these are extremely difficult to discuss in conjoint or even individual sessions.

1. What do I want the outcome of this crisis to be?
2. Can I give up my relationship to the other person?
3. Why did I engage in this affair?
4. Is it wise to explain my motives?
5. How do I regard my experience?

Janice never wavered about wanting to stay married. The possibility that Henry ultimately would choose to divorce terrified her. Although she said she could give up the relationship immediately, she longed to communicate with her ex-lover. I explained to them that both should realize that having been involved for over a year, Janice was *quite attached* to this man. Grief was to be expected. I thought it was a dangerous mistake to act as though it were not happening. Henry quickly reversed his firm position by telling Janice and her paramour that they could talk in order to help Janice to end their relationship. Janice reported that they spoke briefly on the telephone and texted each other for two days and stopped. When specifically asked during the month, Janice revealed that she missed her paramour. After one month, she reported that she was thinking about him far less and did not miss him during Henry's recent absence. She missed Henry!

Janice often tried to explain why she engaged in the affair. Words did not come easily. She acknowledged that she had grown comfortable with sex over the course of her marriage and no longer found it to be dirty. She nodded in agreement when I asked her if their pattern of marital sexual behavior left her somewhat bored. She was curious what it might be like to be sexually involved with another person. The excitement of this relationship was far greater than she ever imagined—*I loved being pursued!* She told herself that she would be disciplined and discreet, that one day the relationship would end of its own accord and her husband would never know. She was shocked to discover how easy it was for her to conduct the affair. She had always thought that she could never be the kind of person who would do such a thing. She was mortified that her husband found out and profoundly guilty about the pain she caused him. She was ashamed of herself. When the questions returned in individual and conjoint meetings about why the affair occurred, she changed the subject to her concerns about Henry's mental health. Janice told Henry that she was telling the whole truth, but it was apparent to me that she minimized the frequency of sexual contact with her paramour and she withheld from Henry much of the process of her missing her lover. It was clear that she did not want to discuss the feelings that she had about the coach or her grief in any other way than to indicate progress. She cancelled each of the two sessions that she asked for in order to better understand her motives for this.

Did Janice love the coach? Certainly not in the way she loved Henry. But can we imagine the pleasure, interest, sexual desire, and caring about him that she felt over the course of their year of daily contacts? She was, as Henry once said in passing, *really into him*. I take that phrase to mean that each of them was preoccupied with the other even when apart.

Love affairs are severely limited by their clandestine nature and the obligations to the family. Individuals generally cannot act upon the full natural expressions of love available to the unattached. They often feel that they cannot afford to even mention love to their paramour. The love is discerned nonverbally by one another. The affective processes of an intense frequent sexual relationship occur regardless of the absence of statements of love. A vital aspect of love is internal and private from everyone.

Janice's love for her coach was in her judgment not a matter to be shared with him, her husband, or her therapist. Having chosen to enter this complexity, she resolved to deal with it alone (or at least without my assistance). I respect this. Love is not a subject that most people want to verbalize fully, even to their beloveds. When patients want to discuss their subjective experiences, I am there to help them put the almost inchoate processes into words. Almost everyone seems grateful for the assistance.

When patients' love affairs are clinically discussed without them present, it is common to hear someone invoke the errant spouse's character pathology. I think they actually mean one or two character traits. Without directly correcting the speaker, I refer to the trait rather than pathology or sickness. Immersion in affectively intense situations requires the therapist to be in the moment with the patients. Discussion of past object relationships often seem more relevant to the therapist or to colleagues around a conference table than to the patient. When their eyes say help me, they are asking for assistance for today's dilemma. Colleagues are correct, of course, that object relationships follow patterns that illuminate aspects of their character. I am never quite sure whether the invocation of character pathology in errant spouses ultimately refers to psychoanalytic meanings involving structure of organization of the self or to lay meanings of character that evoke negative moral judgments, as in, *He is a bad character.*

Monogamy and Countertransference

Monogamy is the dominant form of sexual arrangement in the current Western world. Its violation is the most often cited reason for divorce.[5] It is not, however, a universal organizing feature of marital relationships.[6] Many societies support polygamy. In regions where women are scarce, wives may have several husbands.[7] Some individuals in the United States organize themselves into social groups that practice consensual non-monogamy in part to avoid the dishonesty inherent in infidelity.[8]

Clinicians should not to assume that every person has an internalized prohibition against infidelity.[9] This information is not volunteered, so tactful inquiries are required when the patient's private belief about fidelity is relevant. If a person morally considers infidelity to be wrong, the clinician can infer that the unfaithful person gave in to a temptation. Temptations are part of almost everyone's life, even those who deny them. When a clinician asks about the speed of the surrender to temptation of an early love affair, the door is gently opened to the considerations that led to the affair. We should not be surprised when any one person moves beyond monogamy.

In the United States, the dominant public position concerning marital infidelity is that it is wrong, destructive, and a personal moral failing.[10] There is no term for the person who is unfaithful that does not connote a negative social judgment—cheater, womanizer, adulterer, slut, tart, floozy, etc. Even the word unfaithful conveys a strong negativity. Because all mental health professionals begin their training with a disorders paradigm, we tend to assume that all infidelity is a symptom of individual or relationship psychopathology. As one acquires a developmental paradigm, however, infidelity can be seen as a decision that is made after calculating the benefits and the dangers. Pathology may be reflected in how the calculation was made.

Clinicians have personal values about the subject that can creep up and alienate our patients who expect us to remain calm, nonjudgmental, and clear thinking. Some therapists have known infidelity in their parents, siblings, spouses, or themselves. This invariably shapes their internal responses to their patients' dilemmas. Therapists need to be wary of an uncharacteristic authoritative voice that is telling the patient what to do. *Don't have an affair! End the affair now! Your partner is scum! You must divorce! You should have an affair of your own!* Although each of us may think such ideas, our role is to be interested in the person's dilemmas, to clarify the options, to enable the discussion to focus on what the person is thinking and feeling about the present, past, and future. That is all.

What Love Affairs Might Tell Us About Love

Sexual impulses towards others and transient mutual interpersonal temptations are far more common than opportunities to connect to another on multiple dimensions typically seen during an affair of the heart. The erotic souls of both men and women are occasionally restless and looking for more. Marriage after a time may bring discomforting awareness of the self, the partner, or the future. When conditions are right, the opportunity to fall in love is difficult to resist. The early sensations, the zing of sudden attraction may signal the beginning of the process of falling in love. More is required, however. Psychological intimacy greatly facilitates the initial impact of Cupid's arrow. For thousands of years, the exaltation of falling in love has been likened to finding one's missing half. This is the Platonic myth of being united with the half that was cleaved prior to birth. Plato had more abstract things to say about the search for love.[11] His ideas seem to apply to some affairs of the heart. Urging males to have a lot of sex with whomever they please when they are young, he thought that they eventually would discover the experiences were more or less alike. This then would enable the man to move beyond the carnal to love. He saw the essence of love as a seeking of the good, a striving for personal improvement, a yearning towards perfection, a longing for completion. While Freud speculated that libidinal urges directed humans to intercourse, Plato thought the ultimate goal was not sexual fulfillment but the pursuit of the personal discovery of what is of value and what is beautiful in life. The appreciation of this beauty transcends interpersonal romantic love. Such love is a step to something beyond it.

The private internal thoughts, feelings, sensations, and meanings of a love affair are difficult to put into words. It does not seem any more prudent to get lost in Platonic abstractions than it is to become mired in the mundane practicalities of extramarital dilemmas. Somewhere between these extremes lies the person's sense that there is a spiritual fulfillment in a new devotion to another being. In the patient's own way, he or she is discovering the good. A love affair may feel like a transcendence of the self just as the devotion to a new child (the ultimate model for love) does. A new love once again reorganizes one's life, provides a meaningful new role, and makes the other person at times more important than the self. Of course, a person does not have to go outside of marriage to transcend the self and find carnal and spiritual fulfillment. But we have to be open enough to listen to those who tell us that what they feel with their paramour they never felt with their spouse.

The outcomes of many love affairs make the lovers' original judgments appear to have been stupid, impractical, and destructive. Nonetheless, we need to consider the idea that destroying the status quo was what some people were attempting to accomplish for themselves. Why? They may have been trying to destroy, or at least escape from, the limitations that the impediments of love had imposed on them.

Part II of the Compendium of Love's Pathologies lists the factors that limit a person's lovability. The affair temporarily provides a sense of freedom from one or more of these partner patterns. *For better or worse, in sickness or in health, until death do us part,* is a long time to bear the subjective and objective burdens of the relationship. These burdens are typically experienced as stemming from the partner. The partner's patterns are perceived to be recurrent, limiting, enduring, and unlikely to change. An affair of the heart is an escape from what is known about the partner. The original mystery about the partner is gone; new possibilities are perceived to be limited. A person may have already sensed his or her personal withdrawal and yearns to be connected to someone. Because such thoughts tend to create a search for, and responsiveness to others, it does not seem wise to give them voice or, for some individuals, to allow them into consciousness. Love affairs do not require the perception that the partner is bad (although destructive behaviors are not a rarity). It is more that the partner is known—that is, recognized for abilities, inabilities, style, interests, tastes, and interpersonal impact.

Being known is a double-edged sword. While one may seek a love affair after developing a disappointed conviction concerning one's spouse, one may also immerse oneself in an affair because he or she is known by the spouse. Thus, the joke: *The trouble with my spouse is . . . she knows me too well.*

Love affairs stem from the hunger to prove that life's possibilities are not foreclosed. Part III of the Compendium summarizes the impediments that limit the ability to express love towards a partner. An individual copes with a unique combination of these forces within this list. The love affair may have been mo-tivated by the wish to prove that *I was not the impediment. Perhaps it wasn't my partner alone but it was at least us*. Love affairs convey hopefulness, the wish to be vibrantly connected, to be a better person—to pursue the good.

Individual circumstances in love affairs are far too diverse to speak of in other than generalities. For details in a specific case, one must enter into a trusting relationship with the patient so he or she can teach the therapist about the per-ceptions and thinking that enabled the calculation of benefits to be worth the risk. No one is asserting that the calculations are correct, morally justified or will lead to an improved subjective life. But when affairs are seen as attempts to over-come the impediments to love that are inherent in the partner, the self or their interaction, the particular case details become far less important than the human aspiration to find comfort in the self through love.

George had been struggling with intensifying homosexual desire since his last child moved out. His only homosexual behaviors had been two drunken episodes in college. Married to an anorgasmic wife who never seemed to like sex, he sought assistance for depres-sion and anxiety. He wanted to talk rather than take medication. What he wanted to talk about was his discovery of the Internet gay community and the opportunities this represented for him away and in town. His explorations eventually led to homosexual behavior within several evolving but brief personal relationships. These delighted him. His dysthymia and anxiety dissipated. He and his wife had periodic joking conversations about his homosexual desire. She realized that he had become happier. He told her on two occasions that he had had some sexual behavior, and it was very nice. She was dis-tressed by these revelations and issued ultimatums that he knew he would not, could not, follow. He reassured her that he was not interested in leaving the marriage or humiliating her at church by coming out as a gay man. He refused to give up his friendships, how-ever. After two years of continuing marital stability with fewer sexual initiations by him, he met a man who seemed a candidate for a life partner. Their love affair caused him to ask for a divorce, and he came out to his siblings, parents and young adult children. He was in pain primarily because of his wife's sadness, anger, and loneliness. Church members were supportive of both of them. He became preoccupied with the need to live independently and to work out a schedule for him and his lover, who lived an hour's drive away, to share their lives. This proved difficult for a host of reasons but was ultimately understood due to the fact that George's lover had not come out to his family. His need to maintain his independence unraveled their relationship. George was broken hearted. He thought of returning to the marriage. His depression was alleviated by several more brief, intense romantic excursions, and finally he met a man whom he thought was the one. After three weeks, the man withdrew, and George's reaction was so intense that he had a lost week and wanted to go on antidepressants. George's new friends proved to be empathic and supportive throughout his panicky devastation. They told him that he was new at this process. Although still on the lookout for a life partner, he knows that he has to become more independent. "I count my blessings. I am still part of my family.

I have new friends. I am healthy. I even attended a nude social gathering! I never heard of such a thing. It was quite nice. Life is not as sexual as I thought it would be. It is very affectionate, however. But I still want to be part of a couple. I want to love someone. I want someone to love me."

References

1 Squire, S. (2008). *I don't: A contrarian history of marriage*. New York, Random House.
2 Person, E. S. (2007). *Dreams of love and fateful encounters: The power of romantic passion*. Washington, DC: American Psychiatric Press.
3 Levine, S. B. (2006). *Demystifying love: Plain talk for the mental health professional*. New York, NY: Routledge.
4 Levine, S. B. (2006). Infidelity: Basic concepts. In S. B. Levine, *Demystifying love: Plain talk for the mental health professional*. New York: Routledge.
5 Betzig, L. (1989). Cause of conjugal dissolution: A cross-cultural study. *Current Anthropology, 30,* 654–676.
6 Solstad, K. M. (1999). Extramarital sexual relationships of middle-aged Danish men: Attitudes and behaviors. *Marturitas, 32,* 51–59.
7 Crook J. H., & Crook, S. J. (1988). Tibetan polyandry: Problems of adaptation and fitness. In L. Betzig, M. Borgerhoff Mulder & P. Turke (Eds.), *Human reproductive behaviour: A Darwinian perspective* (pp. 97–114). Cambridge: Cambridge University Press.
8 Anapol, D. (2010). *Polyamory in the 21st century: Love and intimacy with multiple partners*. Lanham, MD: Roman & Littlefield.
9 Anderson E, (2012). The Monogamy Gap: Men, love and the reality of cheating. Oxford University Press, New York.
10 Smith, T. (1994). Attitudes towards sexual permissiveness: Trends, correlates, and behavioral connections. In A. Rossi, *Sexuality across the course of life*. Chicago: Chicago University Press.
11 Bloom A. (2001). *The ladder of love in Plato's Symposium* (pp. 55–177). Chicago: Chicago University Press.

8

LOVE AND SCIENCE

All sexual behavior—solitary or partnered, socially acceptable or immoral, normal or abnormal—is constructed from biological, cultural, psychological, and interpersonal elements. This clinical principle is comprehensive, but it is not esoteric. It merely guides our understanding that sexual problems have more elements that clinicians address in their various therapies.[1] When reading the work of those who have investigated love with scientific methods, the same principle comes to mind.

While sexual behavior and love can be dissociated from one another, they are frequent traveling companions. Romance is a vehicle that propels individuals to sex. Sex is a vehicle that travels towards love. Their intersection creates memorable life-changing experiences. Scientists study sex or love in cross-section at a single moment in time, often eliciting reflections about past experience. Clinicians, when not dealing with its emotional casualties, may observe love as an ongoing process among their psychotherapy patients. The two groups share interest in a central practical question. *What determines how the private processes of sex and love evolve over time to produce happiness, boredom, or misery?*

Social scientists have created a large body of work on love. Its existence makes it all the more curious why there is a paucity of discussion of the topic among those who devote themselves to clinical care. Two ostensible factors may discourage clinicians from the topic. The first is the inconsistent vocabularies of love. These are apparent not only when comparing theologians and scientists but among the social scientists themselves.[2,3,4] The second is that scientifically supported ideas about the pathologies of love suggest etiology, such as impaired early life attachment bonds, but not pathogenesis. They do not provide for a new clinical approach.

The Difference in Emphasis

Research in this arena aims to detect common tendencies to think, feel, or behave lovingly among large samples of individuals. Characterizing the specific love phenomenon under scrutiny is more important than the individual research subject's responses. For example, when Passionate Love is the subject of

95

investigation, the goal is to characterize its subjectivity and its neural correlates. One person's experience with Passionate Love could not be a sufficient scientific basis for its characterization. By aggregating the responses of many, Passionate Love is given a definition that distinguishes it from other forms of love. Clinicians, in contrast, immerse themselves in the subjectivity of individuals one at a time. They find themselves providing care for those deeply disappointed in love, or watching a love process evolve through its increasing complexity. Outcome may be more important to them than the characterization of the former intensity of Passionate Love. Clinicians, however, do not see an abundance of patients during its positive phase. Patients in a passionate state of love come to us when they are unhappy or desperate or fearful of being abandoned. *I think I am crazy* is often heard during the early portion of an extramarital affair, for instance. *I just can't stop myself*. Researchers and clinicians inevitably view love from differing perspectives. The researchers' role is to generate knowledge. Our role as clinicians is to ameliorate mental anguish and minimize its untoward consequences. We assume that the more we understand the sources of anguish, the better we will be able to discharge our responsibilities.

Many Nonprofessionals Understand Love

Before the social and behavioral sciences became interested in love approximately 40 years ago, the subject was the providence of poets, novelists, songwriters, theologians, and philosophers. Their contributions still are likely to provide most individuals with what they grasp about the nature of love and its evolution throughout the lifecycle. Individuals learn about love's possibilities, disappointments, and dilemmas through stories,[5] whether these stories are conveyed via television, movies, novels and short fiction, or orally by friends or family members. However enriching, such learning is very different from the knowledge provided by science. Science provides us with landmarks of love and its bodily underpinnings. Stories tell us about obstacles and dilemmas and provide us with cautionary tales. Science tends to study new love among the never married. Stories may concern love at any phase of the life cycle.

Science is Arduous

It is difficult to scientifically establish any new fact. The scientific process begins with a question. The scientist has to creatively devise an experiment to investigate the answer. The measurement of the data has to be trustworthy. The findings have to be interpreted correctly. The answer to the question is tentative until subsequent studies, often by other investigators, confirm the findings. Ideally, this body of work generates a new theory for further refinement or fits nicely into an existing theory. Every step along the way is subject to intense scrutiny by the investigators and colleagues. Among scientists a theory has little standing until it is tested and supported empirically.

Clinicians have it far easier. Their conclusions, however, are far less certain. Clinical perceptions are based on inconsistent methods from one observer to the next and from one patient to the next. Clinicians' observations are filtered through their values, ideologies, and life experiences. Nonetheless, they frequently observe patterns, tendencies, and relationships between elements in a person's history. Clinically derived hypotheses can provide behavioral scientists with observations to study. That is the extent of the contribution of the clinician to the scientific process.

Questionnaires are a frequent method of gathering data in studies about love. Researchers often devise their own self-report measures.[6] A complex methodological sequence is necessary to create a questionnaire that reliably measures what scientists intend it to measure. Even well established self-report measures have sensitivity and specificity limitations. For instance, scientists need to be careful not to generalize about love to the life cycle when their samples are largely late adolescents and young adults. More complicated means of data generation, such as the fMRI, have many technical artifacts and limitations, not the least of which is differing quality of the machines used from study to study producing different degrees of visual resolution. Advancing concepts in neuroscience can raise doubts about earlier findings. Scientists create an international community and influence each other's thinking and experimental designs. Their work receives far more scrutiny, criticism, and group stimulation than clinical observations. Clinical work often generates case histories of narratives of feelings, behaviors, and processes[7] that are filtered through existent theory.[8] Scientific work generates theories and taxonomies.[4]

It seems logical that any study of love should begin with a clear definition of love. This is not actually the case, however. *What is love?* Agreement exists that the answer to this question cannot be provided within a single sentence. Nonetheless, all findings eventually lead back to this fundamental challenge of defining the subject. Love, a conceptual noun, has been characterized in numerous ways—an ambition, an ideal, an illusion, a capacity, a force of nature, an emotional state, an attachment, and a process—falling in love, intrapsychic meaning making, caregiving, and sexual access. Discussions about the nature of love employ abstractions, intrapsychic shifts, morality, emotions, and behaviors.

A Clinician's Synthesis Provokes Science

From the perspective of Darwinian evolutionary theory, love is a complex suite of adaptive mechanisms, rooted in brain function but shaped by current and remote cultural circumstances. Feelings of love are universally found among human beings. Previously, some thought love was a cultural artifact that was constructed by social forces. Love is much more than an emotion. Its manifestations are thought to exist in order to facilitate survival and reproduction of the human species.[9] Evolutionary biology stresses that the intersection of biological and cultural forces create the forms of love.

1. Love is a set of evolved innate decision biases that affect what we pay attention to, how we interpret events, what we retrieve from memory and how we decide to establish a powerful social bond that enhances reproduction. Innate decision biases are the basis for motivations and cognitions.
2. These decision biases differ for men and women. Females make a higher investment in the bond than males.
3. Love has four recurring domains of decision biases: finding a mate, keeping a mate, caring for offspring, and maintaining friendship. The motivations for these functional modules are distinct.
4. Decision biases in one individual interact in a dynamic way with other individuals. Love is interpersonal.
5. Love bonds are influenced by considerations that derive from larger social fields; the analysis of contingencies that lovers face is informed by considerations beyond themselves, such as historical era, religious sensibilities, and law. One culture may organize love quite differently than another. The need to be in love, for instance, may be weaker or stronger from one society to another.
6. There are considerable cross-cultural variations in the expression of social bonds involving monogamy and various forms of polygamy. These have evolved to solve social problems faced by ancestors in specific regions and cultures.

Perhaps the most important original stimulus for academic interest in love was the clinical work of John Bowlby. His publications, beginning in the late 1970s, provoked an interest in empirically testing his views on the importance of the infant-caregiver bond to the course of life. Bowlby viewed attachment, caregiving, and sex as innate neural motivational systems that ensured infants' survival so that they could pass on their genes later in life.[10] The infant's attachment to its caregiver was seen as the product of the child's tendency to seek comfort and the caregiver's ability to provide it. Bowlby perceived this basic process to be operative in subtle ways throughout life. The emotions associated with falling in love, with loving someone over time, and with losing the partner stemmed from the original attachment process. Infants were thought to have a definable attachment style—secure, avoidant, or anxious. Research on college students indicated that these three styles were still evident in early love relationships.[11] Research in monkeys confirmed the importance of the quality of the maternal-infant bond for adolescent sexual adequacy and social acceptance.[12] Bowlby emphasized how the infant responded differently to accumulating experiences with successes and failures in its quest for comfort and security. The neural system was continually programmed in response to these experiences.

The child's developing brain seemed to be answering three questions, *Is the world a safe place or not? Can I trust my relationship partner in times of need? Do I have the resources to bring my partner close to me?* The answers were thought to ultimately generate various adult behavioral styles that *might* create pathologies of

romantic love. These pathologies can occur through hyperactivation of motivations to secure attachment (desperation) or through self-protective deactivation
of attachment behaviors (resignation). These same responses, hyperactivation
or deactivation, are thought to apply to other domains of love, such as caregiving and sexual behavior,[13] even among rhesus monkeys.[12] A secure human attachment is associated with relationship stability, intimacy, satisfaction, conflict
resolution, commitment, support during stress, positive feelings during sex, and
heightened feelings of love.[14,15] The seminal concepts of psychoanalyst Bowlby
have been repeatedly confirmed by empirical work. The basic concept that is supported is that the capacity for love is rooted in the brain but individually shaped
by life experience. Neuroscientist and opera scholar Zeki reached the same
conclusion in his integrative examination of brain activity and opera themes.[16]
Others have similarly emphasized these points based on the vital resonance between newborns' primitive limbic system and mothers' biological rhythms which
program the child physiologically and create the quality of the maternal-infant
bond. This is referred to limbic resonance.[17]

There are important sex differences in how love operates. Men have been
demonstrated to fall in love at first sight more often than women.[18] An evolutionary explanation for this is that fecundity is critical to men in mate selection.
Reproductive value is associated with female attractiveness.[19] A woman is most
interested in a man's ambitiousness, industriousness, drive, and status and less
interested in his physical appearance because of her life tasks. Young women tend
to link sex and love far more than do young men. Love occurs in the context of
long-term mating. Evolution has provided a reward system within the brain that
generates reproduction—mate selection, sexual union, devotion, and loyalty.
This has not been demonstrated in terms of separate brain physiology yet.

The brain circuitry of love also has the capacity for duplicity, jealousy, and
violence. Women use sex to gain love and men use loving words and behaviors to
gain sex. Clinicians refer to this as the capacity to manipulate. Jealousy is viewed
as a subtle manifestation of love even though it can shatter a relationship. It is a
warning signal that protects a mate from would be intruders or relationship rivals.
While the loss of love creates intense pain in both sexes, it is primarily males
who are likely to threaten or to become homicidal under these conditions. In
one typical study, 33% of murdered women were killed by their intimate partner
in contrast to 4% of men who were killed by a wife or lover.[20] The same neural
capacity for love leads to both ecstasies and horrors.[21]

Dopamine and the Reward System

The most popularized scientific works on love have generated the concept that
there are neuroanatomical and neurochemical bases for Romantic Love. The
constellation of emotions, motivations, and behaviors of this form of love have
now been described by scientists and Plato, documented in questionnaire and
card sort studies, and demonstrated by Shakespeare, famously in *Romeo and Juliet.*

Science has established that the intense sexual desire, obsessive preoccupation, and the wish to be together of Romantic Love do not vary by age, gender, sexual orientation, or ethnic group.[22] The brains of 17 subjects, ages 18–26 years, who reported being in love an average of 7.4 months were studied with fMRI while they looked at a photograph of their lover and a neutral photograph followed by a distraction task.[23] The most significant finding was activity in the right ventral tegmental area and caudate nucleus. These areas comprise the neural network associated with pleasure, general arousal, focused attention, and motivation to pursue rewards. Another group of investigators also selected 17 individuals who were "truly, deeply, and madly in love" but for an average of 28.8 months.[24] Activation was found in the same two areas.

Fisher continued her work employing fMRI with rejected lovers. Her group found activation in the right nucleus accumbens/ventral putamen/pallidum/lateral oribital cortex and anterior insular/operculum.[25] These are part of the reward system as well. Other fMRI studies have demonstrated similar activations with taking big risks, physical pain, obsessive/compulsive behaviors, and ruminations. Over time, as protest over being rejected fades and resignation sets in, there is reduced activity in these areas.

Romantic love's brain regions have a dominant neurochemical substrate—dopamine. Serotonin (lowered levels) and noradrenaline (higher levels) are also likely to be involved. This line of investigation is not suggesting that romantic love is completely explained by its location or its transmitter. Neither is it suggesting that drugs that increase or decrease these neurotransmitters be tried to enhance love processes. Love in the brain is more complicated. Other areas are activated as well, and the dopamine dominance of romantic love is not unique. The reward pathways are also activated through maternal behavior, eating and drinking, social behaviors, general exploratory behaviors, grief, and stress.[26]

Oxytocin, the pituitary peptide stimulus for labor and breastfeeding, can activate these brain regions. Circulating levels increase during sexual arousal and orgasm, dancing, and spiritual activities. It is generally thought to be a prosocial hormone.[27] Endogenous opioids play a role in maternal-infant caregiving—labor and breast feeding. There is also the more familiar subject of the role of sex steroids during arousal or romance. Although many physicians recommend sex steroids based on extensive clinical and laboratory research, where, when, and how they operate in the brain is awaiting scientific elucidation. Brain physiology, which involves numerous circuits, neurotransmitters, peptides, and other hormones, is a more daunting subject than love. Nonetheless, there are those who are already anticipating the day when physicians will be able to prescribe a nasal spray of oxytocin or other agents to enhance or diminish love of another.[28]

Fisher's description of Romantic Love includes: focused attention, euphoria, craving, obsession, compulsion, distortion of reality, personality changes, emotional and physical dependence, inappropriate behaviors, tolerance, withdrawal symptoms, relapse, and loss of self-control. She raises the question whether Romantic

Love should be added to the list of common addictions.[29] Its early phase, Passionate Love, has long been described as an addiction to the partner and sometimes as crazy love. Here is how Hatfield and Rapson described it: "A state of intense longing for union with another . . . a complex functional whole including appraisals or appreciations, subjective feelings, expressions, patterned physiological processes, action tendencies and instrumental behaviors. Reciprocated Passionate Love is associated with fulfillment and ecstasy. Unrequited love brings emptiness, anxiety or despair.[30]

Plato posited that the brief passion of falling in love was akin to the sense that one has finally found one's missing other half.[31] Plato's enduring concept makes us think that the phenomenon is universal. The science of love is largely based on American samples, raising the concern whether scientific conclusions would apply throughout the world.[32]

Types of Love

Bersheid[33] proposed that four types of love exist, each with different behaviors and causes:

- Attachment Love—the most basic one, required for survival manifested by the seeking of closeness to a protecting person.
- Compassionate Love—concern for another individual's welfare.
- Companionate Love/Liking—friendship based on rewards and punishments.
- Romantic Love—distinguished by sexual desire.

Others have called Companionate Love agape, altruistic love, brotherly love, and communal love. It underlies the adult form of Attachment Love. Later in life, it is the basis for caregiving to others in distress, particularly one's parents and spouse. Bersheid suggests that to understand the evolution of love, research needs to specify which of these four forms of love is being studied.

Another taxonomy, The Triangular Subtheory of Love, posits that love consists of three components: intimacy, passion, and commitment.[34] Commitment first involves the private conclusion that one loves another and then the subsequent decision to maintain the relationship with the person over time. From these three elements, seven types of love are classified:

1. Friendship = Intimacy without passion or commitment
2. Infatuated Love = Passion without intimacy or commitment
3. Empty Love = Commitment without intimacy or passion
4. Romantic Love = Intimacy and passion without commitment
5. Companionate Love = Intimacy and commitment without passion
6. Fatuous Love = Passion and commitment without intimacy
7. Consummate Love = Intimacy with passion and commitment

Sternberg emphasized that these seven types apply to one person. Two partners in a relationship may have different types of love for each other. When they are in the same type of love, they may have differing intensities of psychological intimacy, sexual desire, and personal commitment. An individual's mental representation of his or her degree of felt closeness, sexual interest, and commitment and his or her behavioral expressions along these same dimensions do not necessarily closely match. Many empirical studies support these ideas. These ideas reverberate with the complexities of love described by clinicians.[7,8]

A third taxonomy, that of Hatfield and Rapson, separates Passionate Love from Companionate Love. I previously defined their formal concept of Passionate Love. Here are their alternate terms: crush, obsessive love, head-over-heels in love, infatuation, and being in love. They characterize Passionate Love as "hot," meaning accompanied by intense sexual desire. In contrast, they describe Companionate Love as "warm"—a mixture of affection and tenderness for a partner. Their alternative terms for Companionate Love are true love or marital love.[35]

A Tentative Summing Up

In this chapter alone, nine adjectives preceded the word love: Attachment, companionate, compassionate, romantic, passionate, consummate, fatuous, empty, and infatuated. Mention has been made of friendship, liking, falling in love, and being in love as well as numerous alternatives for the nine dominant adjectives. The largest challenge of love requires yet another term, staying in love. Lust, a well-known but inconstantly described depiction of a type of sexual desire or the state of intense goal-directed excitement, has remained unmentioned but lurks within the fluctuating vocabularies of love. Eros has been avoided because of its philosophical and theoretical usage.

As a clinician interested in the pathogenesis of suffering, I struggle to put these terms into a coherent perspective. I hope others will soon improve upon my following synthesis.

1. **Where does love exist?** It exists in four places: within the mind of the individual, in the behaviors of the lovers, within the minds of others about the couple, and within the brain. Scientists and clinicians tend to dwell on the individual's mind since the research subject or the patient is the major source of information. But clearly, when two people love one another, their mutual attitude reorganizes their lives, dramatically changes their behaviors when alone and in public, and grants privileges from which others are excluded. Family, friends, and even strangers know this about a person. Relationship status is one of the first things we want to know about adults. All of this is both too obvious and too complex to dwell upon. However, the fourth locus of love, our brains, is relatively new to our collective awareness. There, love exists as a set of innate context-specific capacities complete with behaviors, motivations, cognitions, and affects.

102

2. **How does love begin within the individual?** In various ways—either with: liking and friendship; flirtation based on physical attraction, admiration, or respect; falling in love; or sexual behavior. If love ensues, it will be referred to as Romantic Love. Romance is a *process* between two individuals that is based upon an ideal of a partial unity or fusion of the two individuals. Romantic Love is an *intrapsychic state* marked by a remarkable emotional investment in the other.

3. **What is the relationship between falling in love and Romantic Love?** The process of falling in love typically aims to initiate the development of Romantic Love. Falling in love results in a new sense of self or sense of identity in terms of the other when it occurs in the widely advertised two-person version. When it is reciprocated, falling in love is among the most pleasant processes of the life cycle. Imagination and idealization are important ingredients of this process. These intrapsychic processes result in the creation of an internal image of the other as *my beloved*. After the brief joyful process is completed, the result is the establishment and maintenance of a highly positive internal image of the partner. As long as this image remains, the person represents him or herself as being *in love* with the partner. Being able to privately experience oneself as in love with the partner is a basic requirement for Romantic Love over time. The persistence of Romantic Love implies a continuing respect for the partner as having a set of highly desirable character traits. In its beginning, Romantic Love is associated with strong sexual desire. Sexual desire, however, diminishes over time in response to numerous factors even when its other ingredients are still in place. One can have Romantic Love even though sexual desire has dissipated.

4. **Does falling in love require reciprocation?** No. Stimulation of imagination and idealization can occur without the beloved's awareness. Several features have the reputation for stimulating the intrapsychic transformative process known as falling in love. Beauty and other outstanding assets, such as skill, intelligence, wealth, status, and athleticism are known to provoke it. Whether one-sided or reciprocated falling in love occurs, it usually occurs within a person who is longing for a social change. When individuals fall in love with iconic cultural figures, they usually have no expectation for reciprocation of Romantic Love.

5. **What is the relationship of falling in love to Passionate Love.** It is the first and most exuberant form of Romantic Love. The fundamental meaning of the word passionate is extreme or intense. Passionate is often employed to describe types of music, language, belief, grief, teaching, collecting, etc. *She is passionate about her art collection.* When falling in love creates the intense desire to be with, know more about, have sex with, and to share the near future with another, this early aspect of Romantic Love is labeled Passionate Love. When Passionate Love is invoked in research settings, sexual excitement

about the partner and sexual desire for the partner are assumed. Clinical experience suggests three cautions about the research assumption.

a. **Passionate Love may have boisterous and quieter forms.** All occurrences of newly felt love would not meet Fisher's description of Passionate Love. Perhaps these men and women who may feel quite happy with their new partners should be described as having fallen in love and passed quietly into the state of Romantic Love without the required intensity of Passionate Love. They are neither addicted to nor feeling or behaving in a crazy way. Their early love experiences include all the ingredients without the boisterousness. They do Passionate Love in their own characterological way; they do not generally behave exuberantly. Their lack of boisterousness does not mean they do not feel deeply about their new love. Deeply is an alternate way of saying intensely or passionately. Whatever its subjective and behavioral styles of expression, however, Passionate Love will evolve into Romantic Love if nothing else deteriorates the relationship between the lovers.

b. **Passionate Love witnessed by clinicians is often due to obstacles to loving.** The most intense Passionate Love states that I get to witness are usually associated with a formidable barrier to realizing love. The barrier may be jealousy or panic stemming from a dramatic fear of losing the partner. A forty-year-old patient of mine, for instance, loved a woman but could not decide to marry her. When she announced her engagement to another, his love immediately became consuming. He felt he would commit suicide if he lost her, so he made his desperate pitch. His sincerely felt I-can't-live-without-you-marry-me scenario succeeded. His Passionate Love receded to happiness, became distracted by wedding plans, and soon after marriage lost its sexual ardor. Falling in love with a married person or being married with children oneself can intensify the feelings of early love and create the desperate edge that makes it seem like an addiction. *I think I am going crazy. I am acting crazy. I'm going to lose my family. I don't want to hurt my children but I can't stop thinking about and seeing this beautiful woman. We are going to get caught!* Of course mental health professionals' experience with Passionate Love, like researchers', is based on limited samples.

c. **Passionate Love can be induced at any time in life through the threat of loss.** Serious illness or death can intensify love so that an individual begins to feel an intensity of need for, admiration of, and celebration of the beloved. A cancer diagnosis may induce a new state of Passionate Love. Some individuals only achieve the conviction that they love their partner when disease or accident threatens the continuity of the relationship. This later-in-life phenomenon is not typically associated with intense sexual desire because of the weakened state of the partner. New romances in the last expected decades of life may have a passionate

104

quality stemming from gratitude for having one last chance at love even though the couple's sexual function is impaired. Finally, many have ironically observed that death is able to induce a Passionate Love for a mate who was not treated with passion or respect in life.

6. **What does new reciprocated love mean to the individual?** When a person becomes aware that *I am my beloved's beloved,* sexual devotion to one another's pleasure affirms their importance to the other. You are wonderful, beautiful, my love, my life, I will always be true, etc. may be verbalized, but these sentiments are expressed during lovemaking without words. The partners accredit one another in this way as invaluable, as beloved.[36] Their resultant happiness is a celebration of love for all to see, admire, and long for.

7. **Where does Consummate Love fit in?** Sternberg's term Consummate Love incorporates the processes described above as well as Bersheid's Attachment Love. Consummate Love allows for major stylistic differences in how a person loves both privately within the self and how the intense positive regard of the beloved is expressed. In Western cultures, Consummate Love is the thought to be the ideal way to begin a marriage and pursue individual fulfillment. (This expectation was not apparently as widespread in Eastern cultures where the self is measured more by success in fulfilling the needs of others.[37,38] The world, however, is becoming a more interactive place.) What is so engaging about Sternberg's model is that it is based on the idea that love evolves as a result of the interaction of each partner's degree of friendship or psychological intimacy, sexual desire or passion, and extent of commitment. I view psychological intimacy and sexual behavior as the two subtle systems of nurturance that partners provide for each other while Consummate Love exists.

8. **How does Consummate Love evolve into Companionate Love?** The answer is through countless mechanisms. It is not possible to exaggerate the importance of this question to those interested in love, be they researchers, clinicians, or those who seek to understand the course of their own lives. Companionate love is the stage that consists of psychological intimacy or abiding friendship but no sexual desire and typically no sexual behavior. (This is not what Hatfield and Rapson posit about Companionate Love![34]) In my view, Companionate Love has two general forms. Companionate Love can be a positive development in that is characterized by the maintenance of respect for, enjoyment of, and caring about the partner. It can last for decades terminated only by serious illness and death. The intensity of pleasure, interest, and caring of this form of Companionate Love will fluctuate as a person becomes aware of their limited future. Like Consummate Love, there is a natural fluctuation of appreciation of what exists. Companionate Love is commonly observed when one or more of the following factors are

present: advanced age, long duration of the relationship, or physical illness. The transition from a quietly evolved state of Consummate Love to one of Companionate Love is often created by an organically induced sexual dysfunction. The new dysfunction gradually makes sexual behavior emotionally unsatisfying for both partners. Their sexual behavior disappears, with or without discussion. The PDE-5i medications seem to be able to assist some couples to avoid Companionate Love, at least for a time. In a similar fashion, agents that increase vaginal lubrication and diminish painful intercourse delay the onset of Companionate Love.

A second form of Companionate Love occurs among young and middle-aged couples. It is an ominous development because it often leads to the loss of the two nurturant systems within the relationship. While this can come about because of organic sexual dysfunction, physical illness, or mental illness, mental health professionals are more apt to be involved with relationships whose asexuality has been brought about by negative psychological and interpersonal processes. In an ideal world, understanding the pathogenesis of early-onset Companionate Love would be the common task of individual, marital, sexual, family, or couples' therapists. Although not usually stated in this fashion, psychological ideologies are attempts to understand the premature loss of Consummate Love.

9. **How do we understand the early development of Companionate Love?** My answer is not through any particular ideology! I want to first look carefully at the surface of what a person or a couple says about their experience with the partner. I want to think about what they emphasize in terms of what mental health professionals have observed over the course of their clinical experiences. I also want to get a sense of each person's individuality—style, capacities, temperament. The surface can demonstrate a great deal. I neither want to demean what the patient has told me as superficial aspects of the real problem nor dismiss what I know about the destructiveness of a person's mishandling of key moments in the relationship. I abide with the surface dynamics because I want to prevent the errors that come about from a too-quick descent into remote explanations. These risk inadvertently bypassing how the asexual state developed. There are individuals, after all, who live quite close to the surface. Not everyone is profound even though they are complex. The clinician's task is often to answer the question in such a way that the patient or couple nods in assent to the sequence of pathogenesis of their new asexuality.

The Compendium of Love's Pathologies suggests to clinicians that Companionate Love be examined through two separate lenses. One lens brings into focus behaviors that may have diminished the lovability of the partner. The other brings into focus the affective and cognitive processes that that may have robbed the person of his or her sexual desire for the partner. One or both of these lenses explain to the couple and the therapist how their sexual system of nurturance atrophied. Being able to specify the pathogenesis of their asexuality provides some hope and gives the couple a therapeutic goal—work through the identified obstacles. When both the sexual nurturance system and the psychological intimacy nurturance system are atrophied, the couple's love qualifies for the label Empty Love. The couple may view their obstacles to psychological intimacy and sexual behavior as insurmountable. Empty Love is the prelude for extradyadic sex, love affairs, termination of the relationship, or grim endurance.

References

1 Levine, S.B. (2007). The first principle of sexuality. *Journal of Sexual Medicine*, 4, 853–854.
2 Lewis, C.S. (1960). *The four loves*. London: Jeoffrey Bles.
3 Lee, J.A. (1973). *The colours of love: An exploration of the ways of loving*. Don Mills, Ontario: The New Press.
4 Sternberg, R.W. (2006). *The new psychology of love*. New Haven: Yale University Press.
5 Coles, R. (1989). *The call of stories: Teaching and the moral imagination*. Boston: Houghton Mifflin Company.
6 Hatfield, E., & Sprecher, S. (1986). Measuring passionate love in intimate relations. *Journal of Adolescence*. 9, 383–410.
7 Person, E.S. (1989). *Dreams of love and fateful encounters: The power of romantic passion*. New York: Penquin Books.
8 Kernberg, O. (2012). *The inseparable nature of love and aggression: Clinical and theoretical perspectives*. Washington, DC: American Psychiatric Publishing.
9 Kenrick, D. (2006). A dynamical evolutionary view of love. In R.W. Sternberg, *The new psychology of love* (pp. 15–34). New Haven, Connecticut: Yale University Press.
10 Bowlby, J. (1988). *A secure base: Clinical applications of attachment theory*. London: Routledge.
11 Hazen, C.S. (1987). Romantic love conceptualized as an attachment process. *Journal of Personality and Social Psychology*, 52, 511–524.
12 Suomi, S. (2003). How gene-environment interactions can influence emotional development in rhesus monkeys. In C.B. Garcia Coll, *Nature and nurture: The complex interplay of genetic and environmental influences on human behavior and development*. Mahwah, NJ: Lawrence Erlbaum Associates.
13 Shaver, P.M. (2006). A behavioral systems approach to romantic love relationships: Attachment, caregiving and sex. In R.W. Sternberg, *The new psychology of love* (pp. 35–64). New Haven: Yale University Press.
14 Brennan, K.A., Wu, S., & Loev, J. (1998). Adult romantic attachment and individual difference in attitudes toward physical contact in the context of adult romantic relationships. In J.A. Simpson and W.S. Rholes (Eds.), *Attachment theory and close relationships* (pp. 394–428). New York: Guildford Press.
15 Waite, L.J. (2001). Emotional satisfaction and physical pleasure in sexual unions: Time horizon, sexual behavior, and sexual exlusivity. *Journal of Marriage and the Family*, 63, 247–264.

16 Zeki, S. (2008). *Splendours and miseries of the brain: Love, creativity and the quest for human happiness*. London: Wiley-Blackwell.
17 Lewis, T., Amini, F., Lannon, R. (2001). A General Theory of Love. New York, Vintage Books.
18 Buss, D. (1989). Sex differences in human mate preferences: Evolutionary hypotheses testing in 37 cultures. *Behavioral and Brain Sciences, 12*, 1–49.
19 Sugiyama, L. (2005). Physical attractiveness in adapationist perspective. In D. M. Buss (Ed.), *The handbook of evolutionary psychology*. Hoboken, NJ: Wiley.
20 Greenfield, L.R. (1998). *Violence by intimates*. NCJ-167237. Washington, DC: U.S. Department of Justice.
21 Buss, D. (2006). The evolution of love. In R.J. Sternberg & K. Weis (Eds.), *The new psychology of love* (pp. 65–86). New Haven: Yale University Press.
22 Fisher, H. (2004). *Why we love: The nature and chemistry of romantic love*. New York: Henry Holt.
23 Anon, A., Fisher, H.E., Mashek, D.J., & Strong, G. (2005). Reward, motivation, and emotion systems associated with early-stage intense romantic love: An fMRI study. *Journal of Neuropsychology, 94*, 327–357.
24 Bartels, A., & Zeki, S. (2004). The neural correlates of maternal and romantic love. *NeuroImage, 21*, 1155–1166.
25 Fisher, H.E., Brown, L.L., Aron, A., Strong, G., & Mashek, D. (2010). Reward, addiction, and emotion regulation systems associated with rejection in love. *Journal of Neurophysiology, 104*(1), 51–60.
26 O'Connor, M. F., Wellisch, D.K., Stanton, D.L., Eisenberger, N.I., Irwin, M.R., & Lieberman, M.D.(2008). Craving love? Enduring grief activates brain's reward center. *NeuroImage, 42*, 969–72.
27 Flanagan-Cato, L.M. (2012). Are you responsible for your hormones? Review: of Paul J. Zak's *The moral molecule: The source of love and prosperity*. *Cerebrum*, July–August.
28 Wudarczyk, OA., Earp, BD., Guastella, AJ., Savulescu, J. (2013). Could intranasal oxytocin be used to enhance relationships? Research imperatives, clinical policy, and ethical considerations. Current Opinion in Psychiatry 26(5):474–484.
29 Fisher, H. (2006). The drive to love: The neural mechanism for mate selection. In R. J. Sternberg & K. Weis (Eds.), *The new psychology of love* (pp. 87–115). New Haven: Yale University Press.
30 Hatfield, E., & Rapson, R.L. (1993). *Love, sex, and intimacy: Their psychology, biology and history*. New York: Harper Collins.
31 Singer, I. (2009). *Philosophy of love: A partial summing up*. Cambridge: MIT Press.
32 Hatfield, E., & Rapson, R.L. (2009). The neuropsychology of passionate love and sexual desire. In E. Cuyler & M. Ackhart (Eds.), *Psychology of social relationships*. Hauppauge, NY: Nova Science.
33 Bersheid, E. (2006). Seasons of the heart. In M. Mikulincer & G. Goodwin (Eds.), *Dynamics of love: Attachment, caregiving, and sex* (pp. 404–422). New York, Guilford.
34 Sternberg, R. (2006). A duplex theory of love. In R.J. Sternberg & K. Weis (Eds.), *The new psychology of love* (pp. 184–199). New Haven: Yale University Press.
35 Hatfield, E., & Rapson, R.L. (2006). *Love and sex: Cross-cultural perspectives*. Boston: Allyn and Bacon.
36 Bergner, R. (2005). Lovemaking as a ceremony of accreditation. *Journal of Sex & Marital Therapy, 35*(1), 425–432.
37 Hsu, F.L.K. (1981). *Americans and Chinese: Passage to difference*. Honolulu: University of Hawaii Press.
38 Chu, G.C. (1985). The changing concept of self in contemporary China. In A.J. Marsella, G. DeVos & F.L.K. Hus (Eds.), *Culture and self: Asian and Western perspectives* (pp. 252–277). London: Tavistock.

9

LOVE AND THERAPY

At the beginning of this book, I asked the question, *If we deemed it important, what would we teach our trainees about love, its problems, its archetypal psychopathologies, and how concepts of love can be effectively used in psychotherapy?* It was not simply a rhetorical question. The purpose of the book was to develop cogent answers to this four-part question. I, of course, deem it important to teach about love not only to trainees in the mental health professions but to experienced clinicians and interested others. I take advantage of the young by singling them out for instruction, but *all* readers should realize that the struggle to understand love is important for *all* of us regardless of our years of experience. We *all* seek to grasp the meanings of love in general, to our work, and in our private lives.

What to Teach Our Trainees About Love

Although I recognize that skepticism is the soul of science, I don't approach the topic of love with an utter degree of it. A clinician who does not doubt, who wholeheartedly buys the narrative of the patient, teacher, and treatment manual and who thinks that mental health professionals' understanding of life processes is distinctly superior to that of other educated persons is probably naïve. Even as trainees aspire to master current knowledge, their skepticism is to be encouraged. Therapists strive throughout their careers to learn how to be effective. At my end of the professional life cycle, trustworthy clinical knowledge seems modest and tentative. Many of the requisite facts from my remote professional credentialing have been replaced by a new set of provisional knowledge. Young mental health professionals, particularly psychiatrists, no longer earn their livings in private practice. They often are salaried by institutions where love as a topic is never mentioned. I hope I can clarify how love is professionally pertinent to them in their institutional work. They are typically in the formative stages of mate selection, relationship maintenance, or family building so that concepts about love are also personally relevant to them. Here are a few injunctions and concepts about love for their consideration.

1. **Love your work.** The professional relationships that you are having with patients require many responses from you that are similar to the best elements of love relationships. These elements are usually discussed under the heading of ethics or professionalism rather than directly referencing love. Professionalism requires that you must act at all times for the benefit of the health of the patient.[1] The boundary between you and the patient must be clear and consistent. Your general goals are to foster independence, growth of capacity, self-understanding, and respect for others even as you are focusing on the more immediate matter of symptom relief. Your honesty must not be questionable. You must deliver upon what you can realistically promise, and you must give the patient your best effort to be of meaningful assistance. You must remain interested in what your patients' think, feel, and understand about their lives by establishing a confidential, largely one-way psychological intimacy between yourselves. These respect-worthy aspects of professionalism also characterize good parenting. They are similar to how the growth of love is sustained within intimate adult pairs. Intimate pairs ideally have a two-way psychological intimacy that facilitates the maintenance of their sexual behaviors.[2] This is how intimate life and professionalism differ.

   The word love in the recommendation to love your work means to make a profound emotional investment in it, allow your identity to be remade by it, respect its capacity to enhance your life, and allow it to be a consideration in all that you do in the future, in and outside your workplace. This sounds very similar to a committed love relationship. For over a century, mental health professionals have periodically likened their work to a form of love.

2. **Love being a student.** It is the source of the personal pleasure of becoming. Plato advanced the idea that love was the seeking of the good.[3] While this is a little vague, it may mean seeking to be better, to become more than one is, to strive to improve. Defining one's professional identity as a lifelong student of the alleviation of patients' mental suffering is not to be equated with formal continuing education. Continuing education is just one means of being a lifelong student. Lifelong learning in the Platonic sense recognizes that the current state of therapeutics is far from ideal.[4] It requires as well an attitude of openness to new perspectives and a thoughtful skepticism about their actual contributions so that you don't uncritically jump on the numerous passing bandwagons. Most of us were eventually exhausted by our formal education and the work required to prepare for board examinations and recertification hurdles. Love being a student means something else.

   Others perceive us to be educated, professional, skillful, and knowledgeable. They think we have useful esoteric capacities. Such esteem for our accomplishments is based on our admirers not having access to our subjectivities. We know that we don't understand how to relieve much of the suffering that patients bring to us. We know some of the relief we provide is not permanent. In large part, our patients hold us in high regard because of our efforts. When it comes to our patients evaluating the results of our work with them, many realize that their lives are more complicated than the treatment of their symptoms can ease.

Love being a student means loving the learning that comes from immersion in patients' lives and the relationships with us that unfold over time. Love being a student is taking pleasure from the development of the self. These two suggestions—love your work and love being a student—unite to generate a behavior towards patients that in other circumstances has been called agape by theologians[5] and Compassionate Love by behavioral scientists.[6] Compassionate love is described as seeing to the welfare or needs of another while seeking little in return. Health professions' ethical principles ask licensees to behave as though they grasp that they are entitled to one tangible and one intangible reward for devoting themselves to the improved health of patient: a fee for services rendered and the personal satisfaction of relieving physical or mental suffering. During the therapy process, it is expected that the therapist will avoid establishing dual relationships with the patient. Violating this guideline, such as treating the patient and becoming a funding source for the patient's new business venture, is frowned upon.[7] Keeping medical or mental health care unencumbered by this pattern is based on much past experience that suggests that dual roles put quality care at risk. The avoidance of dual relationships enables the professional form of Compassionate Love to exist.

Love being a student can be extended to being a lifelong student of love. It is possible to progressively have a better grasp of how love is maintained or destroyed over time. It is possible to eventually know more clearly what love is, and this knowledge can improve one's effectiveness with some patients.

3. **The reason not to talk directly about loving the patient.** Love is employed in numerous contexts. Its meanings can only be discerned in relationship to the context in which it is used. I love that book, I love baseball, I love you son, I love you wife all invoke different aspects of the investment in something outside the self. Each context, however, has the capacity to transform the person in some subtle way and to create a new piece of identity. Professionals understand that sexual and romantic sensations arise in the context of the doctor-patient relationship. In much of our work, we prefer to pretend that the patient does not experience these sensations about us. Most of the time we are safe in this assumption. Boundary maintenance requires that we keep our romantic and sexual responses to our patients' private from them and that we not act upon them. Not act upon them means that we do not deliberately facilitate the intensification of their sexual excitement. We can, however, ultimately use our subjective sexual or romantic impulses to advance our work by recognizing that these feelings often parallel the patient's feelings toward us. We may then respectfully inquire about their experience of us. The reason we don't reference our romantic or sexual sensations about

our patients is that we do not want to mislead them into thinking that an actual two-way intimacy with sexual behavior and pervasive functional attachment is possible. (This is the ultimately negative dual relationship.) We provide the ingredients of loving relationships without focusing on our attraction towards, fantasies about, and felt connection to the patient. It is an act of kindness to maintain our boundaries. Our Compassionate Love for the patient may contain elements of Romantic Love and Consummate Love, but these are to be kept within the therapist's privacy. We are paid a fee to do this; it is part of our culturally expected skill set. Society pretends that professionals do not have erotic responses to patients despite that fact that such countertransference has been discussed in our literature for over a century.[8]

4. **Patients talk about love; be interested.** Therapists have a set of cognitive filters through which we pass patients' complaints and histories. The usual first filter is the diagnostic paradigm of DSM-5. The initial evaluation generates a diagnosis and a recommendation for medication, some form of psychotherapy, or both. The next filter through which the patients' conversation will be passed is usually dictated by the type of therapy the clinician thinks that he or she is conducting—behavioral, cognitive behavior, psychodynamic, motivational, interpersonal, psychoanalytic, etc. Clinicians may consider their ideology to be sufficient to understand and assist the patient, but time generally proves this assumption to be incorrect. A subsequent cognitive filter is represented by one of the following questions. What is going on here? What is generating this problem? Why is this happening? In the past, this filter was labeled a dynamic formulation. The trouble was that most therapists had great difficulty answering the question in a manner that was directly helpful to the patient. I have tried to replace the expectation for a dynamic formulation with the concept of pathogenesis of this patient's problem. A step-wise approach can advance the goals of therapy. I don't want to oversell the focus on pathogenesis. It will not always relieve the symptoms, interest the patient in how to remain well, or demonstrate the effectiveness of the doctor's work to the family, but it will engage many patients in therapy. The focus on pathogenesis slowly removes some of the mystery of their symptoms and helps to clarify their internal impediments to loving.

    Knowing that individuals want to be loved and often do not perceive that they are suggests that the clinician explore the possibility that the symptoms bear a relationship to frustrations in the sphere of love. These frustrations may involve difficulties in establishing a relationship, coping with a partner's unlovable traits, or the internal processes that preclude feeling love for the partner.

    Pay close attention to the implications of what the patient talks about in terms of intimate relationship experiences because this often puts the patient's symptoms in a new light. Rather than cataloguing the symptoms using the DSM cognitive filter, wonder whether the appearance of symptoms or their intensification has any relationship to what is happening in the sphere of love. The appearance of a new unexplained anxiety symptom in a person often turns out to be generated by the growing sense of unhappiness with or disrespect for the partner. While some patients quickly want to discuss what is happening in their lives, many others dwell on their symptoms and have to be encouraged to discuss their life processes. Many modern treatment approaches do not encourage interest in pathogenesis. They are rationalized as being based on etiologies. For these practitioners, the patient has a diagnosis that is best treated with a specific approach such as a medication or cognitive-behavioral therapy. All else is irrelevant. An excellent example of such an approach is found in clinical research projects that try to find out if treatment X is superior to placebo treatment. The patient is in the study because he or she has the required diagnosis. Once the patient qualifies for the study, the focus is on the treatment outcome in the two groups. If X is superior to placebo, the clinicians provide X and tell themselves that their treatment is evidence-based. This type of clinical and research activity belongs to a medical model. There is good reason to be skeptical about such research as a guide to clinical work in the mental health professions.[9] The studies rarely are able to address the individual issues that the patient brings to the therapist.

In our clinic, it is apparent that physicians who offer only pharmacotherapy have significantly higher rates of drop outs, missed appointments, requests for new doctors and higher accounts receivable than those who are interested in the patient beyond their symptoms. These physicians either gradually fill their case load with patients who only want such care, adapt to patients' complaints by providing interest in the processes of their lives, or move to a different setting. All patients, heterosexual, gay, lesbian, or transsexual, talk of their love processes in courtship or in established relationships. Be interested.

5. **Love is many things.** Love begins as a widespread cultural ideal with a strong personal ambition to attain it. Individuals' sense of what is possible in love changes with experience. At the onset of their partnered lives, they are more apt to expect the ideal: partners are expected to accompany, assist, stabilize, and enrich them as they experience life's expected and unexpected challenges. While all partners disappoint the cultural ideal, they do so in very different ways after varying lengths of time.[10] Courtship usually leads to commitment as a result of repeated psychologically intimate conversations. Partners share their subjective experiences, aspirations, and willingness to cooperate on important tasks. Their privileged sense of knowing one another is facilitated by their sexual behaviors. Many disappointments in love relationships induce the loss of psychological intimacy, which in turn diminishes the frequency and satisfaction from physical intimacy. Disappointments in love, perceived departures from the cultural ideal, and realizations that the ambition has been thwarted convert the upward positive interactions of these two forms of intimacy into a downward spiral leading

to anxiety about the future. Occasionally, a mental health professional is called.

Love is also a management process. With time, the demands of a relationship become increasingly complex. More matters are considered in assessing the character, capacities, and compatibilities of the partner than in the beginning of their relationship when they possessed Consummate Love. Psychotherapists listen to many resentful complaints about their patients' partners. Sharing their disappointment in therapy is actually a coping device so that they can remain judicious in their approach to the partner. Some patients are less than prudent in voicing their complaints and trigger the hardening of their partner's heart. It is important for clinicians to remain cognizant that each partner is engaged in a management process that is continually assessing the character, capacities and compatibilities of the partner. We can then help our patients to appreciate the complexity of the circumstances they are in. It is not just their views that determine their relationship fate. Most interventions involve one patient, so the person's views tend to dominate the clinician's mindset. Sometimes, it is far easier to see a couple together to appreciate how their mental lives are determined. When clinicians recall that love is a management process, it is a short step to realizing that many individuals mismanage their relationship.

One day I heard myself telling a self-preoccupied man who complained of his wife's sexual withdrawal and indifference to his concerns that it did not seem that she was acting lovingly towards him. (Lovingly was my word!) Grim-faced, she hard heartedly interjected, "I am raising our children—mostly alone." How did you manage to create this? I asked him. (Pathogenesis) Before he could gather his thoughts, she said, "Its Steven, Steven, Steven all the time." (Narcissism as a character trait) Our conversations then focused on their varying explanations on how this intimacy-less life came about (Each person is a meaning maker). I offered my view of love's ideal several times, stressing how each had failures to accompany, assist, stabilize, and enrich the other. He repeatedly said that he loves her very much and knows that she, in her own way, loves him. I told him that I thought that love was less a speech and more a series of acts of compassion, comprehension, and accommodation. (A functional definition of love.) I explained that long-term relationships have a shifting balance between I, the person, and we, the couple. I asked this college-educated couple if they knew of Martin Buber's I/Thou relationship concept. She glared at him.

---

6. **Where love exists in therapy.** For the mental health professional, the patient's visit may be one of eight that day. For the patient, the visit may be the only one this week, fortnight, or month. Of course, it can mean much more to the patient than the clinician. To most observers, therapy occurs in the private office, for a definable period of time for which the insurance

company, government, or patient pays a fee. There is another view of therapy that specifies that it exists in a different place for a very different amount of time and requires no additional fee.

Therapy takes place in the patient's mind, potentially day and night, when awake and when asleep. It consists of reactions to what the clinician and the patient had said during the session. Mental conversations occur between the two of them at unpredictable intervals between formal sessions. These conversations merge with dreamy fantasies about the doctor that may range between articulate rage and affection or images of loving physical intimacy. When the therapist is able to create a relationship that honors the patient's subjectivity, labels affective states, clarifies their sources, and expands the patient's perspective, safety, hope, and trust are created. The barriers to experiencing these three affects are worked through between sessions by processing much aggression, fear, and misunderstanding. When they are worked through, however, the patient's internal private world is likely to generate ideas such as I really like my therapist, I think my therapist is neat, I wish I had someone in my real life like my therapist, I love to be with my therapist, I love my therapist. I imagined a sexual interaction with my therapist. Clinicians would be wise not to indulge themselves in the notion that such transference responses only happen in psychodynamic or psychoanalytic sessions. This illusion is a reflection of the therapist's disinterest in the patient's internal process or the patient's disinterest in sharing these internal processes.

Loving the therapist is a response to the therapist's consistent provision of psychological intimacy. The clinician is attentive and nonjudgmental while grasping the meaning of the patient's offerings. The clinician often can clarify what is being said by succinctly summarizing it. The clinician seems to enjoy the privilege of being spoken to by the patient. These listening skills bond the patient to the therapist and create an eagerness for the next session. It also allows the patient to look forward to the private mental conversations before the next session. Where does love exist in therapy? Within the patient's mind between sessions.

Occasionally, a patient shares these feelings with the therapist, particularly if the therapist inquires about it in a calm respectful manner that allows the patient to realize the normality of the process. This, of course, increases the trust and respect for the therapist and advances the process further. The classic circumstance involving love of the therapist is the male therapist-female patient dyad. It seems much harder for a heterosexual man to express these processes to his male therapist. There is often a focus on working on problems within the hour. Women are likely to tell their female therapists that they love them but are hesitant to share the erotic representations of that love. Many women therapists are uncomfortable about hearing the erotic transferences from their male patients. Much of what any patient feels for a therapist remains a conscious private experience.

115

Love's Problems

The aspiration to find and maintain a warm, stabilizing, mutually caring sexual bond is thwarted by numerous obstacles. One need only to glance at one's family of origin, look at the daily newspaper, or reflect on one day's set of patients to marshal support for this assertion. Clinicians are not in the position to offer assistance for most of these problems. But there are some that we can directly help with, and others for which our commiseration and understanding provide a much-appreciated support. The compendium may be of some assistance in preparing us to recognize how love processes may fail and which obstacles we may be able to help with. It puts the importance of the problems in which we routinely intervene into an accessible perspective. The compendium tells us that there are two great categories of love problems: those that involve difficulty establishing a stable psychological and physical intimacy, and those that attenuate the emotional investment in an established partnership. The sources of the problems in the first category are much easier to recognize than those in the second category.

The private nature of the processes of emotionally investing in a new lover or of renewing an emotional investment in a partner typically takes place away from a mental health professional. When they occur in our current patients, these processes are best discerned with the help of the patient. We are actually more acquainted with the obstacles to loving than the processes of investing in love, but to define them also requires the work of the clinician-patient team. We are given to speculative explanations for the obstacles to love. These are typically driven by our hidden political values or our current ideological beliefs. It requires discipline to stay close to the data that the patient provides to understand the subject. This is why I have emphasized pathogenesis over etiology. Pathogenesis keeps us focused on our individual patient. What is known about the etiology of our patient's disorder should inform and direct our thinking. We have to discover the obstacles to love patient by patient.

Loss of Love in Committed Relationships

Some of the loss of interest in a partner, decathexis if you prefer that term, stems from the meaning given to the partner's patterns of behavior. Many of these patterns will eventually be sensed as either character traits or incapacities. When these realizations do not end the relationship, they diminish the intensity of the investment. Many individual psychotherapy sessions are spent discussing partners' traits or incapacities and their impact on the patient's investment in the partner. By pointing this out, the clinician may enable the patient to gain a modicum of self-respect—*Oh thank you. I'm annoyed all the time. I thought I was becoming crazy.*

The therapist may elect to take one more step after this expression of gratitude— explain an important subtle aspect of lovability. Frequent annoyance with a partner interferes with the index partner's ability to experience the mate's lovability. It is far easier to love a mate when that person displays happiness in the index partner's being. Small transient moments of appreciation evidenced through facial expressions, happy gestures, and laughter reassure the person of the mate's positive regard. The perception that *I am a source of my partner's pleasure* increases the mate's sense of the partner's lovability. It is a positive feedback loop: perceiving that one is the source of pleasure induces the index partner to subjectively feel delight in the mate—that is, feel that the mate is lovable. Partners do also aggravate one another, however, and the feedback loop can turn negative. It is important that the partner not externally react negatively to the partner's negativity since this intensifies the negative feedback loop. This concept suggests that a steady stream of criticisms, frequent irritable moments and expressions of dissatisfaction are bound to erode the index partner's sensations of loving. Many individuals seem to lose sight of this aspect of relationship management. Love in an established relationship can be quite unstable. It is useful to recall with some individuals and couples that the positive feedback loop was originally integral to the formation of their relationship. The deterioration of love is a result of a series of mishandled moments by the partner or the reaction to the partner.

There are other internal sources of decathexis. A person only has a limited amount of energy to invest in a partner. The person has a role to play in keeping the partner happy. The challenge is how to balance this obligation with the need to remain interested in matters outside the relationship. When a vocational challenge, a family member's or a friend's problem, a recreational pursuit, or pornography capture most of the person's psychic energy, he or she may be accused of taking the partner for granted, ignoring the partner, or losing interest. Partners react to this diminished investment and often experience loneliness. A long-term relationship always involves some degree of shifting of energies because of the demands of reality. Partners need to invest themselves in other matters in order to have a reasonably fulfilling life. It is useful to remind patients of this obligation. In doing so, we focus on the partner's need to be loved. *How do you express your pleasure in your partner's being?* Previously, love was defined as a management process, now we may see that it is also an act of balancing various interests.

Relationships easily become unbalanced and need to be repaired. This does not require a therapist. It requires psychological intimacy. This vital restorative process requires talking about one's inner self and respectful listening. Many couples lose the psychological intimacy skills that previously delighted them. This leaves both individuals vulnerable to fantasizing about a better life with another. Infidelities take away the energy from the partner, of course, but there are many other activities that unbalance the distribution of emotional investments in the partner.

Clinicians are distracted from a direct consideration of most love problems by psychiatric diagnoses. We have to use very good judgment about whether to direct our interventions to the diagnosis per se or to the forces that led to the diagnosis. When the clinician decides that assistance should be directed to psychological and interpersonal sources of the diagnosis rather than the symptoms, focusing on the pathogenesis demonstrates what needs to be worked through. Ideally, the clinician attends to both the diagnosis and the pathogenesis. Psychiatric diagnoses, however, do not generally point the clinicians to consider love processes. Love's problems can initiate or maintain psychiatric disorders. Our mental health professional culture's silence about love tends to blind us to its role in pathogenesis of disorders.

A young woman dropped out of a multi-modal treatment for dyspareunia because after her third session with a pelvic floor physical therapist, she realized that she did not respect her husband and no longer desired to be intimate with him. Two years later, she remarried and had no recurrence of the problem. "Back then, I did not understand my problem, but now I see my pain was a way of rejecting him before I realized the reasons for doing so. I don't blame myself. I was young."

The Archetypal Psychopathologies of Love

Archetypal psychopathologies of love are not to be equated with sexual diagnoses. Lifelong erectile dysfunction or female anorgasmia for example, each of which can prevent the formation of a loving attachment, are merely diagnoses. Each of the patterns described below have a range of manifestations. The most extreme patterns created are archetypal psychopathology. Although uncommon, they are not difficult to clinically recognize. They come to symbolize the range of problems and provide a warning to clinicians to be on the lookout for their more common subtle forms. Archetypes create tragedies. They create iconic memories for clinicians. Theater often displays the iconic or archetypal forms of tragedy. The demise of Othello and Desdemona in Shakespeare's Othello is an archetypal representation of the danger of jealousy, the "green-eyed monster."

Violence Toward the Partner from a Rejected Husband

Murder is the ultimate archetypal form. It is rare for a mental health professional to be involved prior to the crime. After the crime, it is a forensic or a corrections professional who is called upon to evaluate the murderer. Clinicians may have seen the man or his spouse because of physical violence or verbal or psychological abuse before, but few are able to sense the unforgettable outcome. Learning from these egregious iconic patterns of domestic violence has spawned programs for women and children caught in its throes. Domestic violence is a crime; there are available legal tools to prevent exposure to a threatening partner. Sometimes these are insufficient. Domestic violence is a manifestation of the larger patterns of relationship cruelty, partner domination, or sexual sadism, and often alcoholism or polysubstance abuse. Previous infidelity on either spouse's part or jealousy may be involved in the dynamics of violence towards wives who have announced the wish to separate. Whether the violence is driven by *If I cannot have you, nobody can!* retribution for the pain of rejection that the man is feeling or a primitive patriarchal sense of ownership entitlement, all members of the family suffer the consequences.

Jealousy

This painful affect is itself another archetypal psychopathology of love. While most individuals can be made to experience this emotion when there is a threat of mate loss to another, the classic problems of jealousy are memorable because of the broad array of tragedies that may ensue: murder, violence, paranoid mental illness, painful obsessive images of the partner having sex with another person, relentless demands for sex for reassurance, and over-control of the partner's social behavior. Jealousy, occasionally referred to as mate guarding, is often understood as combining two fundamental intrapsychic characteristics.[11]

1. Insecure attachment to a mate. Jealousy is an expected response to a credible threat to the continuity of a sexual relationship. Like the jealousy of siblings over the attention of a parent, some jealous adults are merely reacting to what is happening in their intimate lives, while others are chronically insecure in their attachment and are very sensitive to nuances of increased distance from the partner. Jealousy can, therefore, also be a character trait—a problematic one that erodes a partner's ability to feel love. This trait creates a self-fulfilling prophecy that puts both the person and the mate in a psychological prison.

The insecure attachment of the jealous spouse may not be owned as a personal problem. The insecurity leads to blaming the spouse for social warmth, flirtation, or scheming to have a sexual liaison. Paranoid individuals are quite a challenge to help. The insecure attachment may not be only focused on an imagined sexual rival. Children can be viewed as the competitors for the spouse's interest, attention, and energy. The jealous spouse felt much better when he or she was the sole object of his partner's attention. As life becomes more complicated, the jealous person's wish that the spouse exist only for him when he wants her becomes a profound constriction of freedom.

2. Low self-esteem and a private sense of inferiority. These may combine to create a smothering sense of possessiveness and vigilance to insure that no one else is trying to infringe upon the person's property. The subjectivity of jealousy is a miserable feeling state. The word passionate is often used to modify jealousy. Erotic passion has a much shorter half-life than jealous passion because it is not rooted in the sense of inferiority.

Inability to Feel Sexual Desire for a Loved Partner

This archetypal problem is the subtle destroyer of early love. Its tragic outcomes begin with the confusion of the lovers as to why what once was so beautiful, reassuring, and culturally normative has become a source of anxiety, worry, dishonesty, and sexual dysfunction. It does not stop there. If the relationship continues, it predicts a sexual life together that is without joy, gusto, or pleasure. Many relationships don't survive the engagement or the early years of marriage. Marriages may survive if a child is born but every event including pregnancy, lactation, parental fatigue, etc. serves as the cover explanation du jour for the couple's sexual avoidance. This iconic pattern predisposes to infidelities, divorce, and repetition with a second lover or spouse. The seven developmental patterns that can lead to this archetypal outcome were discussed in Chapter Three.

How Concepts of Love Can Be Effectively Used in Psychotherapy

The answer to this practical question begins with the recognition of the importance of being loved and loving as a stabilizing intrapsychic influence. The calming influence of love requires reciprocity; it is a two-person process. Each person must perceive that he or she is the other's beloved for love to have this positive impact. The perception of being loved can be an illusion, particularly in the early years of a relationship before a person develops a better capacity to accurately read between the lines of a partner's behavior. The lack of insight into oneself or one's partner can be useful! Even a misperception can have the stabilizing effect.

A spouse is apt to read the partner's behavior with these questions in mind. *Am I loved? What does my partner actually feel about me? Am I thought of with affection, appreciation, and respect?* Three forces generate the common themes of love in individual psychotherapy:

1. Uncertainty about the nature of love;
2. Awareness that there can be big differences between a person's feelings, behavior, and words; and
3. Recognition of personal disappointments and frustrations about a partner.

Discussion of these themes are held in check by three opposing forces:

A. The previous moral commitment to love one's partner;
B. The wish to appear in a good light to the therapist; and
C. Uncertainty about the meaning of one's unstated feelings and unexplained life circumstances.

It usually does not take more than a few sessions of trust-building to facilitate discussion of the patient's struggles about love. Patients may begin these discussions at the first session when they consider their relationship problems to be the reason for their consultation.

It is up to the therapist to label these struggles correctly. Many of our therapeutic paradigms do not encourage this. We may perceive the struggle to love diagnostically as the ambivalence of the Obsessive-Compulsive person, the

Borderline Personality Disorder, or the worry that accompanies General Anxiety Disorder and consequently focus the discussion on medications. We may dismiss these concerns as epiphenomena of Oedipal or pre-Oedipal processes or of an anxious attachment style and direct the dialogue to childhood. Or we may take the concerns about love as targets to modify with clearer thinking and instruct our patients in the methods of cognitive therapy. There is much to be said about these approaches, but clinicians need to keep in mind that clinical behaviors risk offending the patient and can lead to cancellation of the next visit. It is important to stay with the patients' concerns and appreciate their sensibilities. We should not be surprised when a patient tells us that a comment we made during the previous session disturbed, angered, or otherwise upset him or her. We are interested in what the patient feels about us, even when it is negative. Therapy, after all, should be a model of a psychologically intimate relationship: we are interested in the patient's views and perspectives. We aspire to neither be defensive or judgmental in learning about the patient's reactions to our words.

It seems far better in many circumstances to acknowledge the patient's struggles to love as important concerns. Love is a known stabilizing influence and source of happiness. The patient's symptoms may bear a direct relationship to the perceptions of the partner's less than loving attitude. The therapist can also build a therapeutic alliance by commenting on the fact that the patient's intense ambivalence is unfortunate. Most individuals prefer to have only minor degrees of frustration and disappointment about their partners. It is often taken as a supportive comment when the therapist lets the patient know that many other individuals struggle in this vital sphere of life.

Our skills in labeling mental processes, making distinctions, and illustrating concepts through analogies provide the missing language for patients' struggles in the sphere of love. This book is intended to help clinicians to a higher level of these language skills. Labeling types of love, discussing mechanisms of love, considering the implications for lovability for various character traits, and explaining what you know about the problems of love keep the topic in the therapy even when most of the focus is on another problem. When the subject of sexual desire or arousal dysfunctions is the topic, the absence of a thorough inquiry about love is apt to raise serious questions in the patient's mind about the clinician's knowledge and competence. The therapist need not be embarrassed by a lack of personal command of all aspects of love. No one possesses such knowledge! There are two people in the office working as a team to help each other understand the patient's experience with this major task of adult development.

There are important exceptions to the idea of incorporating discussions about love in professional relationships. Some patients want their love not to be investigated. In previous writing, I suggested that, among other things, that love was a stop sign. I meant by this that some individuals profess love for a mate, act in quite opposite ways, suffer from the impediments to being loved and resist any significant inquiry into the motives for the love. Love as a stop sign is an intense defense against awareness.[9]

Six years ago, a foreign-born and educated 38-year-old engineer briefly returned to India for an arranged marriage. After three normal physical examinations over three years, he accepted a second psychiatric referral for their non-consummation. They were both virgins at marriage and he had had little experience masturbating because of his wish to remain faithful to his future wife. She showers and dresses out of his sight and permits sex only in the dark. Their sexual behavior consists of his mounting and ejaculating quickly on her lower abdomen. She reports to him that she has no fears of penetration and that the problem is his lack of attraction to her. He denies this to her so as not to hurt her feelings. He says that they love each other very much. They are mannerly with each other. They cannot talk about anything personal. "I think about her like she is one of my sisters or cousins. . . . I think I know the source of the problem: I am not attracted to her, although she is voluptuous, because her skin tone is darker than mine." Since adolescence, he has fantasized being with a woman with fairer skin than his. He used to think he was ugly because of his protruding two front teeth. He says he has no interest in ending the marriage or having sex with another woman because he loves his wife.

I just listened. When I was younger I might have said, *What does that mean?* But, now I recognize the idea that, for some individuals at some moments of time with their therapist, *I love my wife* means I am prepared to go no further in exploring my dilemma with you. I have come to respect this and bide my time for another opportunity. Sometimes, it never comes.

Even in cross-cultural circumstances where marriage is organized differently and there are differing expectations for sex, love, and reproduction, the discussion of love and its personal meanings is relevant. The clinician must be the student even as the patient is expecting interventions that will help him to have a normal sexual life.

How can the clinician not think about love even when the patient is not ready to delve into its natural barriers, pathologies, and iconic psychopathologies?

References

1 Markel, H. (2004). "I swear by Apollo": On taking the Hippocratic Oath. *New England Journal of Medicine, 350*(20), 2026–2069.
2 Levine, S. B. (2006). *Psychological intimacy: The pathway to love in Demystifying Love: Plain talk for the mental health professional.* (Chapter 4). New York, Routledge.
3 Plato. Symposium. In S. Benardete, *Plato's symposium* (2001; pp. 1–54). Chicago: University of Chicago Press.
4 Insel, T. (2013, January 23) Assessing the state of America's mental health system. Testimony before the Committee on Health, Education, Labor, and Pensions at United States Senate. Retrieved from http://www.help.senate.gov/imo/media/doc/Insel.pdf
5 Lewis, C. S. (1960) *The four loves.* London: Joeffrey Bles.
6 Bersheid, E. (2006). Searching for the meaning of "love." In R. J. Sternberg & K. Weis, *The new psychology of love* (pp. 171–184). New Haven: Yale University Press.
7 Roberts, L. W., & Dyer, A. R. (2004). *Ethics in mental health care* (pp. 1–16). Washington, DC: American Psychiatric Press.

8 Gabbard, G.O., & Lester, E.P. (2002). *Boundaries and boundary violations in psychoanalysis*. New York: Basic Books

9 Verhulst J, Kramer D, Swann AC, Hale-Richlin AC, Beahrs J. (2013) *The medical alliance: from placebo effect to alliance effect. J Nervous and Mental Disease.* 201(7):546–552.

10 Levine, S.B. (2006). The nouns of love. In *Demystifying Love: Plain talk for the mental health professional* (pp. 1–17). New York: Routledge.

11 Buss, D.M. (2002). Human mate guarding. *Neuroendocrinology Letters*, Special Issue, Suppl. *4, 23*(12), 23–29.

10

WHAT IS LOVE?

This wonderful question goes to the heart of matter, penetrating the many problems with the establishment and maintenance of love. Picture a bicycle wheel with three apparent elements: a tire, spokes, and a hub. Love is found at the hub. It is a force of nature that radiates through the spokes and alights at various places on the tire. The tire is where clinicians meet the problems of love. In this final chapter, the focus is on the hub.

Love is a foundational concept. It is so fundamental that all people make reference to it in their lives, feel its presence and its absence, and look to it as a source of hope in the world. Religions endlessly speak of it and exhort their followers to organize their lives around its various forms. Love is basic to ethics, morality, mating, parenting, and education.[1] It is also basic to long-term therapeutic relationships. It is noteworthy that this abstract concept is impossible to define in a manner that could possibly please all those who have a stake in the subject.

What is love? is a wonderful question, but only for those who don't mind the lack of a discrete answer. Knowing that the answer may be somewhat elusive does not preclude the hope that its pursuit may be somewhat illuminating. Love merges, blends, into other topics. It is because of its fluid infiltrative capacity that it is so vital to our lives. Mental health professionals have historically preferred to create our clinical science paradigms without reference to it. We prefer other explanations for the problems that are brought to us. Consider this quote from medical historians: Disease is always generated, experienced, defined, and ameliorated within a social world. Patients need notions of disease that explicate their suffering. Doctors need theories of etiology and pathophysiology that account for the burden of disease and inform therapeutic practice.[2] Today, our clinical social world may occasionally tip its hat to love, but the discourse quickly moves on.

Many experienced clinicians have a growing uneasiness about the mental health professions.[3] Psychiatrists are avoiding psychotherapy (a derivative form of love), and our biological researchers have failed to generate major therapeutic advances in the serious disorders that they have targeted for a generation. We define new problems, mechanisms, and visualization techniques but not new solutions. We watch with apprehension the emphasis on criteria-based diagnoses that organize most of the education and research today. We seem to over-diagnose fashionable disorders, such as Attention Deficit Disorder and Bipolar Disorder, just as we under-diagnose those that have passed out of fashion, such as sexual dysfunction. One must wonder if our emphasis on diagnosis plays a role in the limitations of our therapeutics over the last century. Given the well known scientific limitations of our categories, there is a basic concern that the identification of a specific diagnosis may not be relevant to the understanding of patients' lives that creates improvement. When individuals are described as having 2, 3, 4, or more comorbid psychiatric diagnoses, perhaps none of them describes the basic matter.[4] The emphasis on diagnosis has an obvious advantage—providing a medication that has a modest chance of effectiveness—and keeps us within the field of medicine where therapy without a diagnosis makes no sense at all.

Our field is in hot optimistic pursuit of finding a medication to enhance cognitive and affective brain function. This search may be based on the assumption that the problems that we witness are largely caused by dysfunctional genes or abnormal development of neural circuitry. We pay lip service to gene-environment interactions and multideterminism and then pursue an understanding of the neurochemical mechanisms. The environmental influences that may be far more determinative than what is occurring in systems of synapses within a far more complex brain are given short shrift or ignored. Increasingly, psychiatric education generates practitioners that identify as biological psychiatrists. Some maintain the idea that they do psychotherapy along with pharmacotherapy in their less than 20-minute visits. Others acknowledge that they do initial assessments to make the diagnosis and then only follow-up medication checks. They send their patients who need psychotherapy to non-MD professionals. Is it any wonder that love as a topic has disappeared from psychiatric discourse?

I have no argument with the study of biological mechanisms of major psychiatric disorders. I support the endeavor. My view is that it is not useful to argue whether biological, psychological, interpersonal, or cultural forces create mental illness, individuals' diverse subjectivity, and relationship problems. I only suggest that we appreciate the artifact created by studying these interacting determinative forces as though they exist in isolation from one another. Conclusions about most psychiatric topics, including love, may be helpful, but they arrive with humbling incompleteness. I just want to clarify what love is and suggest that we honor its location at the hub of human experience, including the experience of suffering.

In the past, I looked at love as if it was a noun but quickly realized it was also an action concept. It was apparent to me then that it was not one thing; it was many things that seemed to blend into one another.[5] I am not certain that I was correct. It may be one thing, one force, one accomplishment that aspires to be permanent but is, in fact, unstable. The thing that it is may only be an attitude—an attitude that has the power to dramatically shift one's behavior and reorganize one's external and internal life. Clinicians and lay persons are, of course, interested in how the attitude of loving another comes about among adolescents and adults seeking it. We can choose from among answers such as these: the magic of Cupid's arrow, the mystery of "chemistry," the wish to be near and possess beauty, the longing for completeness, the judgment that an opportunity for a win-win social arrangement exists, or desperation to end loneliness, Whatever!

We clinicians earn our livings by listening to the anguish of those who cannot maintain the attitude of love. We may study the speculations of others who invent analogies to explain the suffering: good and bad objects coming to the fore and receding, the inevitable consequences of poor early life processes, impulse-driven versus risk-aversive characters. Whatever!

We may incorporate or promulgate new concepts of how to help people with their relationship dilemmas: come clean about the affair, deal with the differences in their levels of differentiation, focus on family of origin issues that are projected onto the partner, analyze their Oedipal conflicts. We may study the defenses employed by patients to maintain the illusion that they are loved and love another in the face of contrary evidence. Whatever! None of this intellectually stimulating, sometimes brilliant work provides an answer to the basic question about love. What is it?

Individuals make assertions of love all the time. Some people say *I love you* when they say goodbye to their lovers in person and on the phone. These social reflexes do not necessarily correspond to feelings of pleasure. They begin in joy and soon become perfunctory manners unique to the couple. Love may be eloquently spoken of but it is not actually a declarative speech. To define love, we must move beyond styles of expression and focus on the emotions that are labeled love. These usually involve felt experiences of pleasure in the interactions with the partner and a consistent degree of interest in the partner's words, behaviors, and happiness. Our partners are ever-noticing the degree of our pleasure and interest in them. A fuller emotional experience of love in its early decades adds the third component to love, sexual desire. Without the development of this component, the relationships belong to other important categories, like friendship, parental love, love of a parent, etc. But these three emotional components are still only part of the experience of love. Two other features are inherent in the attitude of love. The fourth feature is more complex than emotion. It combines devotion to the other, caring about the other, willingness to cooperate with the other, and ease of doing things for the other. I summarize the diverse aspects of the fourth component as dedication. Dedication encompasses devotion, caring, cooperation, and putting the partner's needs before one's own at times. The fifth ingredient of the attitude of love is a judgment that sharing one's future with the partner is much preferred to not being with the partner. It is a private sense of optimism about the partnership. It is what underlies initial and enduring commitment.

The attitude of adult love in its most complete form has five elements, each of which may be thought to exist in differing degrees: pleasure, interest, sexual desire, dedication, and optimism. The reason that love looks and feels so different from one couple to the next and from time to time in the same couple is that these components fluctuate in intensity. When Sternberg's three elements of love were empirically confirmed, it was also recognized that friendship (intimacy), sexual desire (passion), and commitment invariably changed over time in every person.[6] His synthesis that individuals get stuck in labeled negative states of love is correct. Even in these states, however, there is fluctuation. The constant subtle movement of these five elements of love creates uncertainty about love at some time in most individuals. It also generates the desire not to share many of these fluctuations with the partner. The internal instability of love accounts for its external unpredictability. Love can move from happiness to misery and from misery to happiness in rapid or slowly evolving ways. This affords clinicians an opportunity. Awareness that relationship misery can disappear enables some distressed individuals and couples to seek the assistance of mental health professionals.

The attitude of love always evolves. Even though we can't fully understand the conscious and unconscious shifts within a person's mind that initially create love, we know that shifts will continue throughout life. The original shift to the attitude of love, the process of falling in love, is only the most culturally celebrated of love's evolution. It is very easy to tell charming stories about love's beginnings. We like to hear about or see happy individuals who think that they have realized their ambition to identify a partner who will accompany, assist, stabilize, and enrich them throughout life. We can readily feel their joy over finally locating a reciprocated love. We routinely perceived them to be happier, more centered, and less anxious. Thereafter, however, an almost imperceptible evolution occurs that is recognized by changes in the surface of individuals' lives. When does a couple typically not walk side by side anymore? Two years, four years, ten years? Why does this happen? How familiar does a couple have to be with one another in order to lose sexual interest in one another? After 1,000 sexual experiences, twenty years of life together, never? Such questions indicate that there are hidden processes occurring as we stay together. Because clinicians don't generally spend a great deal of time with happily evolving couples, we don't learn about the predictable steps in the evolution of love through the decades. Instead, we are immersed in lives that have many impediments to love without the luxury to research how the normative process went wrong.

In the past, relying heavily on the seminal work of Erikson, Vaillant, and others who had carefully studied adult development,[7] I outlined what I thought were the tasks of adult development decade by decade.[8] The emphasis in my synthesis of their work highlighted the developmental challenges involving vocational skills, health maintenance, financial management, balance of responsibilities to one's partner, children, and parents, and parenting skills. Catching up with the delayed accomplishments of previous decades was present in each decade and seemed to explain a great deal of our individual differences. Love and intimacy were mentioned but given no more emphasis than other developmental lines.

Today, I find myself wondering if one day our field will be able to list the expected developmental features of love and intimacy decade by decade. Now I have only the distress of my patients to deduce what normative tasks of love may have been violated. I try to work backwards to reveal the sequenced pathogenesis of their problem and to describe the developmental challenge that they and their partners failed to master. When I hear about poor money management, post partum depression, arguments that smolder, poor support during illness, and depression after retirement, I think that others must handle these challenges more successfully. Some with the same general circumstances better manage income and expenses, generate consistent adequate support for the mother in the early months of an infant's life, discuss disagreements in a respectful manner and find acceptable solutions, rally to provide sufficient care to the physically ill partner, and take advantage of opportunities afforded by not working. I see all of these tasks of development as potentially influencing one's lovability and ability to experience pleasure, interest, sexual desire, devotion, and optimism about the partner. Love can be sullied by failures outside the developmental line of love. Love's problems are often epiphenomena not just of past developmental difficulties with relationships but also of other contemporaneous difficulties such as work failures, poor judgments about money management, the lack of cordiality to family, etc.

Returning to the bicycle wheel, love's pathologies are located on the tire and love's energy originates in the hub. What do the spokes represent? I suggest that there are two ways of viewing the spokes. The first is that the spokes are where love's ambition is disappointed. It is there that its energy is blocked and distorted by frustrations within the other lines of development. These include sexual and nonsexual sources for the complicated feelings about one's partner. The battle within the patient about the partner occurs along a spoke. The second distorting influence that prevents love from maintaining its positive trajectory over time is the interaction of specific character traits of two individuals. The partners' mundane behaviors, laden with different meanings within each of them, create moments of connection that sustain the conviction that they love one another and other moments of disconnection that add to the uncertainty of their goodness of fit. These character traits interact on the spokes as well. The energy of love is delivered to the tire through the spokes and either creates a relatively smooth surface or a bumpy one laden with affective and behavioral impediments.

The conceptual utility of this analogy is further enhanced by an understanding of the process of psychotherapy. Therapy begins with the presentation of a set of symptoms. These are quickly translated within the clinician's mind into a diagnosis or two. The work of therapy, an emerging grasp of the pathogenesis of the symptom complex, moves the process from the rubber of the tire to the metal of the spoke. Each subsequent session can move down the spoke a bit more. If medication dramatically improves the patient's symptoms, the clinician and patient are typically delighted and the process stops. But if not, the inquiry continues moving, ideally, to the internal or interpersonal situation that seems to explain the bumps on the tire. By understanding and employing concepts about love, the movement down the spokes towards the essence of the symptom-generating process moves more efficiently. The patient and the clinician gain respect for the ambition to love and the destabilizing effects of its private failures. A bicycle has two wheels, of course. The ease and smoothness of its movement, although it can be made arduous by a problem at one wheel, is ultimately dependent on the elements within each of the wheels. This explains to me why marital therapy can be difficult.

Love is a commitment to several important ideas. For most Western individuals, it is a commitment to sexual fidelity. But it is also a commitment to keep from the partner many of the disappointments, resentments, and frustrations of daily life. It is a commitment to protect the partner from the transient, and to behave as though one is consistently devoted to the partner's physical, mental, and social welfare. This means that rather than thinking of couplehood as good or bad, healthy or pathological, we think of it as containing its own dramas involving the intersection of meanings, based on moments, involving both mundane and rare events. As clinicians, we routinely listen to stories of these moments. What do we actually hear in them?

What is love? The question seems to be incomplete without at least a brief consideration of a related one, *What is loving?* I am mindful of the Erich Fromm's 1956 book, *The Art of Loving.*[9] Should love be considered an art form? Like most psychological processes, love has a personal intrapsychic aspect and an interpersonal behavioral expression. Grammatically, love is both a noun and a verb. Behaviorally, it involves acts of understanding, kindness, cooperation, appreciation, protection, companionship, and at times, compassion. Loving behavior also consists of features that are unique to the partnership, such as psychological intimacy, sexual activity, and financial revelation. These are inherent to the arrangement. Psychologically, loving acts correspond to a positive internal sense of the partner, a happily chosen and continuing obligation to the person, and a sense that the two psyches are intertwined and cannot be torn apart without great damage. Some have more talent in the art of loving than others. Some understand the art intuitively, while others can be quite articulate about their responsibility to maintain an attitude of love. Many also intuitively or explicitly understand that although the other dimensions of love inevitably will change over time, their dedication to the partner will last until death. The art of loving has much to do with personal responsibility. There are those who understand and exercise so little of the art that a clinician despairs that any significant therapeutic goals will never be met. But we see far more individuals who need a little assist in understanding the dimensions of love and how they might better put them into practice. We subtly coach them, inspire them to try harder, and keep in mind the consequences of continuing artlessness.

What is love? My answer is it is an invisible force of nature that creates an attitude towards a selected other. The attitude has five important dimensions: the experience of pleasure in the other, a great interest in the other, the desire to behave sexually with the other, dedication to the other, and an optimistic commitment to remain with the other. The vital attitude of love creates a series of expected behaviors that indicate the high value of the partner to the partner. These behaviors are interpreted as acts of loving when they consistently involve cooperation, dependability, kindness, and responsibility.

I am a clinician. My ideas illustrate all the scientific limitations inherent in my role. Like you, I hear many stories. I have gradually come to hear stories differently than I used to. Almost every workday, I am immersed in my patients' problems of love. I am not certain how I functioned in my earlier years when I did not mention the topic very often. I must have perceived stories through different paradigms. I filtered the stories through diagnostic, ideological, or sexual filters. I did notice that many of my patients talked about love at key moments when they were making major decisions about their lives. In my later years, when I began to tell them my thoughts about love's nature and its processes, they often responded with rapt attention and conspicuous gratitude. Sometimes they provided an editorial comment that what I had just said was helpful, that they had never thought of it in that way, or that it seemed to be the essence of the matter. *You hit the nail on the head, doctor.* Many expressed regret that the session was not tape recorded because they feared they would not be able to remember exactly how I said what I did. The most frequent comment when I respond to their stories with a statement about love has been, *Could you repeat that? Do you mind? I would like to write it down.*

Do I mind? Do I mind that you find me helpful when I talk about what is producing your emotional distress? Do I mind that saying what is increasingly obvious to me is experienced by you as illuminating, relief giving, and provides you with a clearer idea about how to represent yourself to your mate or proceed with life? *Certainly, write it down if you think it will be useful.*

What I do mind is the length of time it took me to learn these things. First, I had to allow myself to be skeptical about the limitations of current psychiatric concepts. That required years. I tried to immerse myself in scientific processes long enough to appreciate their strengths, limitations, and role in our field. In doing so, I came to have a clearer idea about the separate strengths, limitations, and role of clinical work. It is my hope that some of what I have conveyed in these chapters will be useful to other clinicians and that they will not have to spend as much time as I did to recognize the importance of love to our work.

References

1 Kleinman, A. (2013). From illness as culture to caregiving as moral experience. *New England Journal of Medicine, 368*(15), 1376–1377.
2 Jones, D.S., Podolsky, S.H., & Greene, J.A. (2012). The burden of disease and the changing task of medicine. *New England Journal of Medicine, 366*(25), 2333–2338.
3 Knoll J. (2013, April). The humanities and psychiatry: The rebirth of the mind. *Psychiatric Times,* 29–30.
4 Blum, L.D. (2013, April). Five key fantasies embraced by DSM. *Psychiatric Times,* 32A, 32G.
5 Levine, S.B. (2006). *Demystifying love: Plain talk for the mental health professional.* (pp. 1–32). New York: Routledge
6 Sternberg, R.J. (2006). A duplex theory of love. In R.J. Sternberg & K. Weis (Eds.), *The new psychology of love* (pp. 184–199). New Haven: Yale University Press.
7 Vaillant, G.E. (2003). *The wisdom of the ego.* Cambridge: Harvard University Press.
8 Levine, S.B. (1998). *Sexuality in midlife.* New York: Plenum Publications.
9 Fromm, E. (1956). *The art of loving.* New York: Harper and Row.

INDEX